Explorers of
the New World

Other books in the History Firsthand series:

The Black Death
Castro's Cuba
The Civil War: The North
The Civil War: The South
The Constitutional Convention
Early Black Reformers
The Gold Rush
The Great Depression
The Holocaust: Death Camps
Japanese American Internment Camps
Life Under Soviet Communism
Making and Using the Atomic Bomb
The Middle Ages
The Nuremberg Trial
The Oklahoma City Bombing
Pearl Harbor
Pioneers
Prohibition
The Renaissance
The Roaring Twenties
Sixties Counterculture
Slavery
The Underground Railroad
The Vietnam War
War-Torn Bosnia
Women's Suffrage
The World Trade Center Attack

Explorers of the New World

Jake Mattox, *Book Editor*

Daniel Leone, *President*
Bonnie Szumski, *Publisher*
Scott Barbour, *Managing Editor*
David M. Haugen, *Series Editor*

GREENHAVEN
PRESS®

THOMSON

GALE

San Diego • Detroit • New York • San Francisco • Cleveland
New Haven, Conn. • Waterville, Maine • London • Munich

LIBRARY OF CONGRESS CATALOGING-IN-PUBLICATION DATA
Explorers of the New World / Jake Mattox, book editor.
p. cm. — (History firsthand)
Includes bibliographical references and index.
ISBN 0-7377-2170-7 (lib. : alk. paper) — ISBN 0-7377-2171-5 (pbk. : alk. paper)
1. America—Discovery and exploration—Sources. 2. Explorers—America—History—Sources. 3. Explorers—Europe—History—Sources. 4. Indians of North America—First contact with Europeans—Sources. I. Mattox, Jake. II. Series.
E101.E97 2004
970.01—dc21   2003049126

Contents

Foreword   10

Introduction: Understanding Exploration Narratives   12

Chapter 1: In Search of a Water Route to Asia

Chapter Preface   35

1. Sailing an Unknown Ocean with an Anxious Crew
   by Christopher Columbus   37
   Christopher Columbus sailed west across the Atlantic
   in hopes of finding a direct route to the wealth and
   riches of the Orient. Neither he nor his crew was certain of what they would encounter in these unknown
   waters. His shipboard journal entries—paraphrased
   and edited by Bartolomé de Las Casas—demonstrate
   Columbus's increasingly anxious anticipation of land
   and his worries about the crew's loyalty.

2. Across the North Atlantic
   by Various Correspondents in England   47
   In 1497 explorer John Cabot convinced Henry VII of
   England to sanction a trip across the northern lati-
   tudes of the Atlantic in search of a route to China.
   Cabot left no detailed account of his journey, but
   contemporary letters shed light on this first recorded
   European exploration of North America.

3. Finding the Straits of Magellan
   by Antonio Pigafetta   55
   The Portuguese explorer Ferdinand Magellan em-
   barked in 1517 on a risky journey to find a route
   through the South American continent, which he still
   thought of as an extension of Asia. In this account,
   Antonio Pigafetta, one of the few to survive the journey, describes the exploration of the South American
   coastline, the discovery of the strait, and the hardships faced when the expedition continued.

4. A World Unknown to the Ancients
by Giovanni da Verrazzano   63
In a letter to the king of France, Florentine nobleman
Giovanni da Verrazzano describes his 1524 explorations, which revealed not a water passage through
to Asia but a continual landmass in North America
from the Carolinas to Newfoundland. His discoveries
contradicted much of what classical scholarship had
assumed to lie across the Atlantic Ocean.

5. At the Mercy of the Winds
by Juan Rodríguez Cabrillo   72
In 1542 Juan Rodríguez Cabrillo set out from Mexico
on a voyage of discovery up the California coast. He
hoped to find a passage to Asia. Instead, as his log
book indicates, the expedition made it as far as Oregon while constantly plagued by the hazards of sea
travel.

Chapter 2: Encountering the Natives

Chapter Preface   81

1. Slaves, Spices, and Gold
by Christopher Columbus   83
In a letter to Ferdinand and Isabella on the return
from his first voyage, Columbus describes the natives
that he met in the New World. According to Columbus, the villagers verified his claims of vast riches in
these new lands, and he asserts that the inhabitants,
themselves, can easily be controlled or pressed into
slavery.

2. "Willing" Christian Converts
by Pedro Vaz de Caminha   92
In 1500 Pedro Álvares Cabral headed a Portuguese
fleet bound for India. In making the wide turn around
Africa, however, his course took him first to the coast
of Brazil. In this account, Pedro Vaz de Caminha, a
writer in Cabral's fleet, describes to King Manuel
what he considers to be the primary source of future
"profit" in the New World—natives ready for conversion to Christianity.

3. A "Golden Age" in the New World?
by Amerigo Vespucci 102
In a letter written to his patron in 1502, Amerigo
Vespucci describes the people and places he explored
in his voyages on the coast of South America. Encountering natives who apparently lived off an un-
spoiled land owned by no king, Vespucci imagines
that the New World is experiencing a "golden age" no
longer known in Europe.

4. In Defense of the Natives
by Bartolomé de Las Casas 109
After arriving in the New World in 1502 and witness-
ing the conquest of Cuba, Bartolomé de Las Casas
turned to speaking out against violence toward and
exploitation of the natives. In his *Short Account of the
Destruction of the Indies*, Las Casas makes the con-
troversial argument that the people of the New World
are human, and he tries to convince the Spanish
Crown to put an end to the crimes being committed.

Chapter 3: Conquest

Chapter Preface 122

1. Power Struggles in the New World
by Vasco Núñez de Balboa 124
Before making his noted "discovery" of the Pacific,
Vasco Núñez de Balboa, leader of a Spanish settle-
ment in Central America, wrote a letter to his king.
By doing so, he hoped to secure his own power in the
New World and protect himself against other Euro-
pean conquerors.

2. A Civilization Deemed Worthy of Conquest
by Hernán Cortés 133
In 1519 Hernán Cortés began his conquest of Montezuma's Aztec empire. His letters to Charles V of
Spain are, in part, an attempt to gain the king's support for his exploits: conquering the advanced Aztec
civilization, searching for fabulous wealth, and colo-
nizing Mexico.

3. Looting the Incan Empire
by Francisco de Xeres   144
In the early 1530s Francisco Pizarro, the Spanish
governor of Peru, began the conquest of the Incas. In
this account, Pizarro's secretary, Francisco de Xeres,
writes of Pizarro's success, his dealings with the Incas, and his acquisition of large quantities of gold.

4. "Blinded and Dazed" by Greed
by Gonzalo Fernández de Oviedo y Valdés   153
This account, based on the diary of Hernando de
Soto's secretary and augmented with critical com-
mentary from the historian Oviedo, describes the violent and mercenary nature of de Soto's 1537 expedition to the territory of La Florida.

Chapter 4: Inland Journeys

Chapter Preface   162

1. The Wondrous Cities of the Aztecs
by Bernal Díaz del Castillo   164
Passages from *The True History of the Conquest of
New Spain* describe Bernal Díaz del Castillo's first
impressions—as a member of Hernán Cortés's invading army—of the city of Tenochtitlán and the Aztec
civilization in Mexico.

2. Traveling with the Indians
by Álvar Núñez Cabeza de Vaca   173
One of only four survivors of the 1528 Pánfilo de
Narváez expedition to explore and conquer the
"virgin" land along the coast of the Gulf of Mexico,
Álvar Núñez Cabeza de Vaca wrote of his growing
sympathy for the natives on his incredible journey on
foot across Texas and through to Mexico City.

3. Negotiating on the St. Lawrence
by Jacques Cartier   181
In his *Voyages*, Jacques Cartier tells of his exploration of the St. Lawrence River and his searches for
the elusive passage to Asia and the rich kingdom of
Saguenay. In this account, Cartier's efforts are com-
plicated by difficulties communicating with the Indi-

ans and by the growing mistrust created by the behavior of the Europeans.

4. **River of the Amazons**
   by Gaspar de Carvajal   190
   The chronicler of Francisco de Orellana's 1541 through
   1542 expedition on the Amazon reports a seemingly
   endless succession of battles with natives, the difficulties of finding food, and encountering a legendary tribe
   of women warriors known as the Amazons.

Chapter 5: Seventeenth-Century Expansion

Chapter Preface   200

1. **Exploring the Spanish Southwest**
   by Juan de Oñate   202
   In his 1598 expedition to explore and colonize the
   territory of New Mexico and convert its inhabitants,
   Juan de Oñate, of Basque Spanish descent but born in
   Mexico, encountered many natives who had already
   met Europeans and were thus not very welcoming.

2. **Making Native Allies and Enemies**
   by Samuel de Champlain   210
   In the early seventeenth century, Frenchman Samuel
   de Champlain founded a settlement in Quebec, thus
   establishing a permanent French presence and expanding the fur trade. He also became involved in
   conflicts between Indian groups and allied with several tribes against their common enemy, the Iroquois.

3. **Navigating the "Great River of the West"**
   by Jacques Marquette   216
   Searching for converts and a river route to the Pacific
   Ocean, French Jesuit missionary Jacques Marquette
   canoed with trader Louis Jolliet and native guides
   down the Mississippi River in 1673. Marquette's account of the expedition emphasizes the explorers' fears
   not only of unknown territory and hostile natives but
   also of the Spanish settlers in the gulf coast region.

Chronology   224
For Further Research   228
Index   231

Foreword

In his preface to a book on the events leading to the Civil War, Stephen B. Oates, the historian and biographer of Abraham Lincoln, John Brown, and other noteworthy American historical figures, explained the difficulty of writing history in the traditional third-person voice of the biographer and historian. "The trouble, I realized, was the detached third-person voice," wrote Oates. "It seemed to wring all the life out of my characters and the antebellum era." Indeed, how can a historian, even one as prominent as Oates, compete with the eloquent voices of Daniel Webster, Abraham Lincoln, Harriet Beecher Stowe, Frederick Douglass, and Robert E. Lee?

Oates's comment notwithstanding, every student of history, professional and amateur alike, can name a score of excellent accounts written in the traditional third-person voice of the historian that bring to life an event or an era and the people who lived through it. In *Battle Cry of Freedom*, James M. McPherson vividly re-creates the American Civil War. Barbara Tuchman's *The Guns of August* captures in sharp detail the tensions in Europe that led to the outbreak of World War I. Taylor Branch's *Parting the Waters* provides a detailed and dramatic account of the American Civil Rights Movement. The study of history would be impossible without such guiding texts.

Nonetheless, Oates's comment makes a compelling point. Often the most convincing tellers of history are those who lived through the event, the eyewitnesses who recorded their firsthand experiences in autobiographies, speeches, memoirs, journals, and letters. The Greenhaven Press History Firsthand series presents history through the words of first-person narrators. Each text in this series captures a significant historical era or event—the American Civil War, the

Great Depression, the Holocaust, the Roaring Twenties, the 1960s, the Vietnam War. Readers will investigate these historical eras and events by examining primary-source documents, authored by chroniclers both famous and little known. The texts in the History Firsthand series comprise the celebrated and familiar words of the presidents, generals, and famous men and women of letters who recorded their impressions for posterity, as well as the statements of the ordinary people who struggled to understand the storm of events around them—the foot soldiers who fought the great battles and their loved ones back home, the men and women who waited on the breadlines, the college students who marched in protest.

The texts in this series are particularly suited to students beginning serious historical study. By examining these firsthand documents, novice historians can begin to form their own insights and conclusions about the historical era or event under investigation. To aid the student in that process, the texts in the History Firsthand series include introductions that provide an overview of the era or event, timelines, and bibliographies that point the serious student toward key historical works for further study.

The study of history commences with an examination of words—the testimony of witnesses who lived through an era or event and left for future generations the task of making sense of their accounts. The Greenhaven Press History Firsthand series invites the beginner historian to commence the process of historical investigation by focusing on the words of those individuals who made history by living through it and recording their experiences firsthand.

Introduction: Understanding Exploration Narratives

The firsthand accounts of the explorers and conquerors that are excerpted and discussed in the following pages represent the period of early European exploration of the New World. Some accounts are from letters directed toward a patron or monarch, others are from books and journals published many years after the events themselves. Others are even taken from books written by sixteenth-century historians, who culled through the narratives of the explorers as they constructed specific histories of the first few decades when the civilizations of Europe and the Americas discovered each other.

The accounts contained within tell the stories of people who often overcame great obstacles and displayed perseverance and courage in exploring the oceans and the newly discovered lands. Less directly, the narratives also tell about the experiences of the natives of the New World in their early encounters with the Europeans. In so many ways, the lands and peoples encountered by the explorers were truly "unknown" to them, representing ways of life, beliefs, and worldviews far removed from those of Renaissance-era Europe. The oceans that the explorers had to cross were equally strange and unfamiliar, and the shipbuilding and navigational technologies of the age afforded little security and assurance that a ship setting out would indeed return.

Yet these carefully crafted stories also represent the outlooks and goals of individuals who were writing for certain audiences at specific times. As such, they emphasize information they deemed important, completely omit other aspects of their experiences, and at times invent details in order to create a specific story of heroism. What remains foregrounded and what remains hidden in these passages reflect not an objective reality that appears the same to different peoples at different locations and time periods. Rather, the documents can be read as demonstrating courage *and* fear; the ability to overcome obstacles *and* the exploitative nature of conquest; and the quest for riches, fame, and knowledge, *and* the violent and brutal treatment of millions of non-Europeans.

Additionally, taken out of context these passages can reinforce the idea that all the resources, ideas, and knowledge necessary for the advancement of civilizations since the sixteenth century have emanated from European sources. Often obscured underneath the accomplishments of explorers, however, are the people, historical conditions, and specific realities that made these journeys possible and whose existence compels us to expand our understanding of the significance of these voyages. These include non-European pre-Columbian explorers who reached the Americas first; the reliance of European shipbuilders, navigators, and explorers on foreign sources of knowledge; and the two-way nature of the exploration of the New World, as Europeans took many new products, types of agriculture, and forms of knowledge back with them to the Old World. Also hidden are the voices of the indigenous inhabitants themselves.

The Heroic Tale

Many of the accounts written from the New World follow a theme of heroism, as the documents emphasize feats accomplished and hardships overcome and downplay or ignore altogether failures and complications. As with all writers, each explorer/conqueror had a specific audience in mind and certain goals in writing, such as seeking support from a monarch for official status and power, trying to obtain the continuation of patronage and the funding of future expeditions, or advocating for a policy change in governance.

In these accounts, heroism frequently becomes the primary focus. For instance, the account of Francisco de Orellana's expedition on the Amazon River in many ways sounds like the script for an adventure film. The beleaguered heroes fight their way through hostile territory not just to survive but also to expand the course of knowledge about this wonderful "new" continent. Similarly, Juan Rodríguez Cabrillo's journey up the California coast, as reported first-hand, is a tale of humans against the elements, with small ships seemingly helpless in the face of the forces of nature.

The Historians Remember

While accounts such as these—if published immediately—may have had a variety of effects on sixteenth-century readers, over the years they have often elicited favorable and ad-miring responses from historians. And just as the stories of each explorer vary widely, the veneration shown to them springs from many different sources. As one example, Amerigo Vespucci has been seen as heroic by at least one historian not only for the dangers he overcame and the endurance he and his crew exhibited but for other factors as well:

> His robust constitution, his proved ability as an executive and manager in the complex business of equipping ships and engag-ing in international trade, his practical knowledge of the materi-als and supplies needed on a protracted sea voyage, his skills in cosmography, cartography, mathematics, and astronomy, his in-telligent and inquiring mind.[1]

Probably the most illustrative example of the heroic sta-tus achieved by many explorers, though, is that of Christo-pher Columbus, whose bravery and valor is often considered legendary. As his journal demonstrates, Columbus and his crew sailed into an ocean of unknown length, with un-charted winds, currents, and climatic conditions. He wrote of his fears that the crew might not remain indefinitely loyal, and he searched vigorously for a passage to Asia that turned out not to exist. Columbus's accounts, and tales written later about him, have inspired many historians. For example, for historian and Columbus biographer Samuel Eliot Morison, Columbus was indeed a valiant hero. "He had [a] firm reli-gious faith . . . the scientific curiosity, the zest for life, the feeling for beauty and striving for novelty that we associate with the advancement of learning," writes Morison. "And he was one of the greatest seamen of all time."[2] The stories Columbus told about himself have, for more than five centuries, been remarkably potent in influencing the stories told by other explorers.

An Incomplete Knowledge of Geography

In telling the heroic tale, Columbus and other explorers also demonstrated to varying degrees both a lack of accurate knowledge about the globe in the fifteenth and sixteenth centuries and the fundamentally hazardous nature of long-distance sea travel. These additional variables add the element of danger and subsequently augment the heroic reputations of the explorers. Contrary to some historical conjectures, explorers during the time of Columbus did not actually believe the world was flat; nevertheless, the state of geographical, astronomical, and technical knowledge was far from what it is today.

The compass had been in use, in one form or another, since at least the twelfth century, thus giving navigators at least some reliable accuracy in terms of direction. But for sailors of the fifteenth century, venturing into an uncharted ocean and losing sight of land still brought grave risks. Although they could tell which way magnetic north was, with no other reference points it was impossible to say with certainty how far in any direction they had sailed, especially after being battered around in a storm.

It was in the fifteenth century that European sailors began to gauge their location and distance based on observations of astronomical bodies, but even this required using instruments that must be held steady on a small ship being tossed up and down on the rolling sea. In the 1480s sailors developed a mostly reliable way of measuring and determining latitude— or one's location on a north-south axis—and this in many ways dictated strategies of navigation, as captains would sail north or south to the desired latitude and then head west in hopes of finding land sooner rather than later.

Accurate measurements of longitude—how far east or west a ship was—were not available until the eighteenth century. Captains and navigators such as Columbus relied on a technique known as dead reckoning to estimate how far they had traveled in one day. This method depended upon the ability of experienced seamen to estimate their speed visually—perhaps by watching how quickly the ship passed by patches of seaweed or driftwood—though these estimates could, of course, be significantly affected by winds and currents. The difficulty of measuring distance traveled, coupled with gross underestimations of the actual circumference of the earth, allowed explorers such as Columbus to reach the conclusion that they had in fact reached Asia—or islands off the Asian mainland—in their Atlantic crossings. It also added to the drama of the narratives produced. Columbus, for example, reported that he manipulated his crew into believing that they had not traveled as far as they really had. He hoped thereby to prevent them from losing their courage and forcing him to turn back. The ruse on his part was facilitated simply because of the difficult and unreliable methods used to determine distance.

Additional Dangers of Sea Travel

Another element that suggested danger and thus contributed to the heroic narrative was the limited geographical knowledge available in contemporary maps and charts. Columbus could argue that he had in fact landed off the coast of Asia because the maps and charts of the time provided very limited assistance. Sea charts had been available since at least the thirteenth century, but for the explorers in the fifteenth and sixteenth centuries headed across the Atlantic, they were especially unreliable and often conjectural and could not give the necessary information about strong and dangerous currents, shoals and reefs to avoid, or the locations of safe harbors.

The harrowing experiences of Juan Rodríguez Cabrillo charting the coast of California and Ferdinand Magellan searching for a strait through South America testify to the hazards of sailing in uncharted waters. As the log of the

Cabrillo expedition reported, his two ships faced many dangers due to treacherous conditions and the lack of known safe ports: "They were forced to weigh anchor again and depart, because there was no port other than the shelter of the islands. The wind shifted. . . . and they sailed around these islands eight days with very foul winds, taking shelter from them under the islands themselves."[3] Even Columbus returned from his first voyage with one less ship than the famous three with which he had started: the *Santa Maria* had struck a reef in the uncharted waters off of the island of La Española (Hispaniola) and sunk.

Adding to these uncertainties was the variable so crucial to sailing: the prevailing direction of the winds across the ocean. For the first few decades of Atlantic crossings, navigators had to discover through experience that winds usually blow one way in certain places and different directions in others. In some locations, known as doldrums, there might be no wind at all, causing great anxiety as disoriented sailors far from home saw little headway being made. If severe storms arose, they could most safely be ridden out by taking all sails down, but this left the ship and crew to drift at the mercy of the waves and currents and take the expedition far off course.

In short, given the difficulties in determining location, speed, and distance traveled, along with the unexpected storms, unpredictable currents, hidden reefs, and the relatively small size of the vessels sent on these explorations (John Cabot's ship, for example, was only manned by approximately twenty sailors), the dangers confronting these voyagers were striking. Adding to these factors for the earliest explorers, of course, was the simple fact that no one knew for sure where land would be found. These uncertainties, when foregrounded either in the firsthand accounts or by later historians, added much to the heroic aspects of the tales of these explorers. As historian John R. Hale observes, "Taking the period of discovery as a whole, an expedition member's chances of getting back alive were probably about 50-50."[4] In such terms, the explorers who reached their goals (or at least reached the New World) defied death and ensured their reputations in history.

The Objectives of the Explorers

Although exploration narratives frequently featured tales of danger and heroism, this strategy was but one element in attaining the larger goals and desires of the explorers themselves. In other words, they were not simply trying to entertain. For instance, after Christopher Columbus's landfall on and exploration of islands in the Caribbean in 1492, he wrote a letter to his patrons describing the "mines of gold" on the island of Española and the land's proximity to the home of the (mythical) Asian ruler known as the "Grand Khan." He may well have believed both of these incorrect assertions. Regardless, though, each served an important purpose for the explorer. First, his promise to his patrons of gold, spices, cotton, wood, and slaves, in quantities "as much as they shall order," would, if true, have made Columbus himself a very rich man. He had negotiated an initial contract with King Ferdinand and Queen Isabella of Spain that granted him one-tenth of all revenues resulting from his expedition as well as the titles of governor of any lands discovered and admiral of the ocean sea.

Second, such a report undoubtedly played an important role in securing for Columbus sponsorship of his second voyage in 1493, a tremendous undertaking of more than twelve hundred men on seventeen ships (as compared with fewer than one hundred men on three ships in the 1492 journey). Had he reported accurately after the first expedition that the new lands were actually thousands of miles from Asia and that he had in fact seen little actual gold, his chances for additional sponsorship would have surely been diminished. Instead, though, the promise of vast riches and the possibility of establishing a settlement that could serve as a crucial trading post near Asia ensured that Columbus would be allowed to return to the New World.

As another example, after Vasco Núñez de Balboa "discovered" the Pacific Ocean off the coast of Panama approximately twenty years after Columbus's first voyage, Balboa wrote a letter back to King Ferdinand. Due to the great distance from the Spanish Crown and its governance, and the necessarily slow nature of communication across the ocean, leaders in the New World such as Balboa often competed against each other in an effort to solidify their own power. Balboa's letter serves precisely this function, as he strategically highlights his own achievements in establishing and governing settlements while telling of the supposed greed and incompetence of his rivals. As he wrote disparagingly of his adversaries in the colonies, "I make known to Your Most Royal Highness that [they] took on so much presumption and fancy in their thoughts that they appeared to themselves to be Lords of the land and from the bed could they rule the country."[5]

In a similar manner, Hernán Cortés's letters to Spain's Charles V during his 1519 conquest of Mexico specifically depict the Aztecs as a civilization worthy of conquest; according to Cortés, Mexico was both a commendable adversary and the home to vast riches that would make attractive spoils. Cortés, who directly disobeyed the directives of the Spanish-appointed governor in the New World by invading Mexico, hoped in his letters to convince the Crown of his devotion and of the incredible benefits his endeavors would bring. In this one account, then, Cortés demonstrated his own heroism in overcoming this worthy enemy, thus helping to secure his own status against his opponents, while providing details he knew would ensure continued interest and support from his monarch.

What the Monarchs Wanted

What the European rulers were interested in hearing from their explorers in large part was information that would solidify their claims to new territories and lead to successful future voyages. Thus, the reports played important roles back in Europe as monarchs competed with each other and explorers vied for current and accurate intelligence on the activities of their rivals.

The different countries of Europe had much in common in the so-called age of exploration. For example, most experienced large population growths during the late fourteenth and early fifteenth centuries, and most people in Europe—perhaps 70 to 80 percent—belonged to the landless peasant class. Each nation had also developed larger merchant classes that could invest the capital necessary to provide ships and provisions for overseas expeditions.

Yet there were important differences among the Europeans who sponsored voyages to the New World. Each European monarch supporting an expedition faced a distinct set of historical circumstances contributing to or, at times, hindering the desire and ability to send expeditions into the unknown. In addition, during this time period the countries supporting the expeditions described in this anthology— Spain, Portugal, England, and France—often held different expectations of what their explorers should accomplish.

Spain, for example, in the time of Christopher Columbus, had recently completed its conquest of the Muslims in the southern kingdom of Granada and expelled its own Jewish population in an effort to increase internal social control. Until such goals had been achieved, Spain's leaders were not able to devote attention and resources to undertakings such as that proposed by Columbus. The explorer had first proposed his idea to Queen Isabella and King Ferdinand during the mid-1480s, but with Spain's attentions and treasury devoted elsewhere, Columbus's venture to find a water route to Asia was delayed.

However, with the 1492 victories over the Muslims, the Spanish monarchs were now more attuned to the advantages that a successful route across the Atlantic could bring. First, they hoped such a trade route could give Spain an advantage over its neighbor and rival Portugal, which had long demonstrated its prowess on the seas (especially in its exploration of the African coast). In addition, such a trade route that Columbus hoped to find would not only be much shorter than the route east by land (especially since Columbus vastly underestimated the size of the oceans and the entire globe), but it would also eliminate any "middleman" traders or rulers controlling territory through which the land routes to Asia passed. Finally, the royal treasury would surely benefit from the vast riches in gold, silver, and other resources that Columbus promised to find in any new lands discovered. For many years Portugal, Spain's rival, had been sending expeditions farther and farther down the western coast of Africa. By 1488 Portuguese navigator Bartolomeu Dias had proven that it was possible to sail from the Atlantic around the southern tip of Africa and into the Indian Ocean, thus connecting Europe by sea to the commerce of India. Pedro Álvares Cabral's voyage in 1500 was officially meant to solidify this link, and King Manuel I sent a fleet of thirteen ships with Cabral to consolidate Portugal's status as a trading power in the eyes of both European rivals and Asian potentates. When Cabral's fleet landed first on the coast of Brazil, having most likely been blown far off course, it was not only an important discovery of a new continent, but it also intensified the rivalry between Spain and Portugal in New World colonization. In a 1494 agreement called the Treaty of Tordesillas, both Spain and Portugal agreed that new lands discovered east of an imaginary line 370 leagues west of the Cape Verde Islands (which are roughly 400 miles off the coast of the northwest portion of Africa) would belong to Portugal, and everything west of that line would be Spain's. Brazil fell under Portugal's control based on this treaty. With the agreement already in effect, the rivalry remained friendly rather than hostile, allowing that "the two rivals could each proceed to rapid colonial expansion without friction."[6] Still, due to difficulties in accurately measuring longitude (a challenge that would not be solved until the eighteenth century) and continued disputes over territorial rights, the two countries remained intensely competitive in staking claim to sections of the New World.

While Spain and Portugal vied with each other for possession of newly discovered lands, other countries, such as England, were slower to mount voyages of exploration and publicize their claims in the New World. Although not considered a major power in European affairs for most of the fifteenth century, in part due to internal conflicts, England began to assert itself under Henry VII's rule in 1485. It was Henry VII who granted permission to Genoan merchant John Cabot to voyage across the ocean in search of new lands to claim and trade routes to Asia that would propel England into the ranks of the European powers. Cabot's 1497 landing in North America is often considered the first official European "discovery" of the continent, though it is probable that fishing expeditions from Bristol, England, had reached Newfoundland during the previous decades.

Like England, France had also been preoccupied with military engagements both internal and external, such as its 1494 invasion of Italy, and it thus devoted less attention to exploration at the turn of the century. The first French royal support of an expedition was provided to Giovanni da Verrazzano in 1523 in his exploration of the east coast of North America, and then again during the 1530s and 1540s with Jacques Cartier in Canada. Although neither undertaking resulted in the establishment of the highly prized trade route to Asia nor the acquisition of vast riches from new lands, the French presence in Canada later provided the foothold for a growing fur trade empire and claims to vast territory in the middle of what is now the United States.

The Scramble for Information

The rivalry among the European nations sometimes meant new opportunities for explorers in search of a patron. In many ways, several explorers—such as Giovanni da Verrazzano, Christopher Columbus, Ferdinand Magellan, and John Cabot—served as "free agents," accepting royal support where it was forthcoming, regardless of whether it was from their native land. Thus, although their discoveries and land claims became the property of the country under whose flag they sailed, the explorers themselves paid great attention to each other and tried to find as much information as possible about routes taken, navigation techniques, and discoveries made.

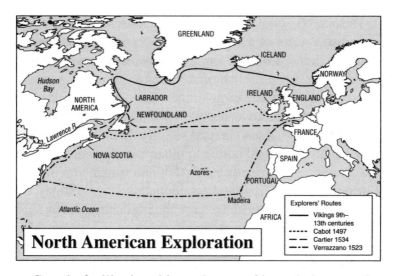

North American Exploration

Explorers' Routes
——— Vikings 9th–13th centuries
----- Cabot 1497
— — Cartier 1534
—·— Verrazzano 1523

Greatly facilitating this exchange of knowledge was the development of printing, which occurred around 1450. Although books were by no means the available and inexpensive commodity they are today, with the advent of printing, merchants, nobility, and monarchs were able to obtain more reliable and consistent information regarding geography, technology, and recent expeditions. Explorers' narratives, then, were not read just for enjoyment; rather, they were in high demand in Europe as intelligence reports for nations seeking to compete in New World exploration and for the explorers themselves, who hoped to learn as much as possible from their predecessors' voyages.

News of John Cabot's expedition to North America, for example, prompted a torrent of letter writing between European diplomats and merchants eager to find some way to capitalize on Cabot's discoveries. One of these correspondents, a Spanish representative in the English court, wrote to Queen Isabella and King Ferdinand of Spain to inform them of their possible rights to Cabot's claims in the New World: "Having seen the course they are steering and the length of the voyage, I find that what they have discovered or are in search of is possessed by Your Highnesses, because it is at the cape which fell to Your Highnesses by the convention with Portugal [the Treaty of Tordesillas]."[7]

Despite objections from rivals, such accounts and histories could serve as a type of "legal" proof of discoveries made in this era when competing powers hoped to outdo one another and establish official claims to newly encountered territories. For example, the wide circulation of news of Columbus's discoveries on his first voyage did not just spread his fame, it also helped solidify Spain's claim to the new lands and served notice to other European powers that the Spanish had arrived first in that part of the New World. Furthermore, the firsthand accounts that survive today are surely matched by those never made available to historians; for at certain times monarchs felt the need to hide valuable geographical information from one another or not let it be known that an explorer in their employ had made a landing in areas claimed by other nations.

Pre-Columbian Explorations

While modern historians believe that many reports from explorers have been lost or were deliberately kept secret by European monarchs, there are other absences as well in the historical record. The heroic stories emphasized the dangers faced and obstacles overcome by the European explorers and conquerors, but they are notable as well for what they leave out. Frequently absent or downplayed in the narratives historians have studied and preserved are references to the contributions of non-Europeans to exploration, technology, European agriculture, and the very survival of many of the exploring expeditions themselves.

The New World was of course not at all "new" in any sense to its original inhabitants. Nor was it necessarily "new" to all outsiders. Some historians have suggested the existence of pre-Columbian journeys of Asian explorers who reached the western coasts of the Americas, for example. Indeed, the Chinese had sent many expeditions during the fourteenth century to the coasts of Africa, demonstrating a curiosity and the technological ability to make dangerous ocean crossings. From within Europe, Norsemen from Scandinavia began moving west to Iceland and then to

Greenland during the eighth century, and they established at least short-lived settlements in the northeastern extremes (and possibly farther inland) of North America within a few hundred years. Further, fifteenth-century expeditions from Bristol, England, were likely undertaken that sent fishermen to the waters off the coast of Newfoundland well before Cabot's journey. And the possibility has been raised that African explorers had crossed the Atlantic as well, as Columbus apparently had heard from different sources that there had been trade between African nations and peoples in South America and that expeditions from across the sea had reached the Americas before him. As one historian has provocatively suggested, the traditional portrayal of Christopher Columbus as discoverer of the Americas has been "a cheap con trick."[8]

The Contributions of Non-Europeans

While Europeans were making important advances in the technological knowledge necessary to complete a voyage across a vast and unfamiliar ocean, their ships and instruments had not developed without contributions from non-Europeans. For example, sailors relied on such instruments as the compass and the astrolabe, but their ships themselves benefited greatly from a change from clumsy square sails to the triangular sail. This improvement, borrowed from Arab seamen, facilitated the building and use of smaller and more maneuverable ships that could more safely navigate through a difficult ocean.

In addition to this type of knowledge crucial for passage to the New World, once there the explorers and conquerors relied heavily on native peoples for their knowledge of geography, their ability to survive in environments that Europeans could barely tolerate, and their willingness to ally with the invaders to defeat other native enemies. For example, Hernán Cortés's vastly outnumbered Spanish army relied on alliances with such peoples as the Tlaxcalans to successfully march to Tenochtitlán and conquer the Aztec Empire. As one historian has written, "There would have been no Conquest without the Indians who recognized and seized the opportunity to bring the Aztecs down that was afforded by the Spanish presence."[9]

As another example, as Álvar Núñez Cabeza de Vaca recognized throughout his writings, his very survival on his remarkable walk through what would later be the southern United States depended upon the kindness of the native peoples he encountered and their abilities to survive off the products of an apparently unforgiving and harsh land. And Columbus himself benefited greatly from the incredible generosity of the peoples he found in the Bahamas and the Caribbean. When the *Santa Maria*—Columbus's vital supply ship—struck a reef and began sinking, the local cacique, or native chief, immediately sent men and canoes to help unload the vital provisions and supplies.

Devastation in the New World

What narratives of heroism and adversity written from the perspective of Europeans also frequently ignore or put in the background are the striking and horrible realities brought by New World exploration. By some estimates, approximately three hundred thousand Spaniards immigrated to the settlements in the Americas during the sixteenth century; the suffering and destruction that they and others brought to the inhabitants of these lands was, by any measure, horrific. In 1519 it is estimated that the population of central Mexico was 25 million people; about eighty years later there were only between 1 and 2 million native peoples remaining because of the wars, epidemic diseases, and mistreatment that Europeans had brought. Entire populations on Caribbean islands were wiped out in a very short time. The roving expedition of Hernando de Soto in the southeastern part of North America left behind vastly altered and weakened civilizations that would decline and disappear within a few generations. As one historian writes, "As a result [of expeditions such as de Soto's] the native societies of La Florida in the early sixteenth century were greatly changed from those observed by Europeans and Americans in the late seventeenth

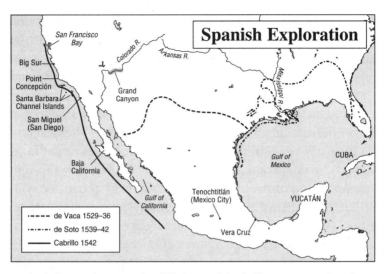

Spanish Exploration

San Francisco Bay
Big Sur
Point Concepción
Santa Barbara/Channel Islands
San Miguel (San Diego)
Colorado R.
Arkansas R.
Grand Canyon
Mississippi R.
Baja California
Gulf of California
Tenochtitlán (Mexico City)
Vera Cruz
Gulf of Mexico
CUBA
YUCATÁN

-·-·- de Vaca 1529–36
-··-··- de Soto 1539–42
——— Cabrillo 1542

and eighteenth centuries."[10] A world of diverse peoples, languages, cultures, and civilizations was quickly being dismantled and destroyed. Europeans such as Cortés and Francisco Pizarro conquered and then systematically destroyed advanced civilizations in their quests for riches and power. The Aztecs that Cortés encountered, for example, were highly organized; adept at building elaborate architecture, roads, and water canals; and skilled engineers and craftspeople. This advanced civilization, which grew out of cultures and empires dating back more than one thousand years, was gone within decades of Cortés's arrival.

In addition to deaths through disease and outright violence, many practices were instituted in the European settlements that brought about great suffering in the quest for riches and converts. For converting the natives was, in effect, the duty of the Europeans, especially the Spanish and Portuguese, whose Catholic rulers had initially been conferred dominion over the new territories by the papacy. Thus, attending to the religious needs of the natives was a primary justification for many practices. For example, the early sixteenth century saw the rise of the *encomienda* system, which was essentially a mixture of serfdom and slavery thrust upon the natives. In this system, legally codified by Spanish law, estates or entire villages were placed under the control of individual Spaniards. The peoples living on these lands were then required to labor on behalf of the owner. In exchange, the native was supposed to receive religious instruction and protection. In reality this system was easily abused, as overseers used brutality, horrible working conditions, and long hours to extract the maximum amount of profit from the mines or agricultural fields of their estates. In his early years in the New World, "Defender of the Indians" Bartolomé de Las Casas had grown wealthy through the operation of his own *encomiendas*. The abuses he contributed to and witnessed under this system surely were an important factor in his "conversion" experience in 1514 and his subsequent writings against continued exploitation. As Las Casas himself later wrote, "Our Spaniards have destroyed the Indians in two ways. . . : disastrous wars which they call conquests and distribution of land and Indians which they present under the veneer of the name *encomienda*."[11] After the Indian population declined precipitously during the sixteenth century due to these types of practices, the continued need for labor in the New World led to the rapid growth of the slave trade from Africa.

Searching for Native Voices

If the depopulation of the Americas often remains in the background of early narratives of exploration and conquest, this was in part achieved by suppressing or misrepresenting the voices of the indigenous inhabitants. Given their inability to successfully repel the invaders, the natives of the Americas repeatedly found themselves treated as slaves or children, whose voices and opinions were of little importance. For the explorers to have foregrounded and demonstrated respect for the perspective of the conquered would have meant recognition of the natives' fundamental status as human beings. It might have implied that although the native cultures and civilizations were vastly different from European standards, that did not mean that Europeans had the right to destroy and conquer them. Of course, no European bent on claiming land and wealth for his nation would admit to the absurd notion that "primitive" peoples had any prior right to New World territories.

In addition, although explorers depended heavily on their abilities to successfully communicate with the indigenous peoples they encountered, differences in language, culture, and ways of thinking often prevented anything resembling a true understanding between parties. Thus, narratives such as that of Jacques Cartier, which include many conversations between Europeans and natives, need to be read with the understanding that what the explorer *thought* the natives were expressing (and vice versa) was frequently only partly accurate. Native words and actions were often conveniently interpreted by the Europeans in ways that furthered European goals and supported their perspectives.

Not only are native voices absent or distorted in the explorers' narratives, but most indigenous accounts of the age of exploration have also disappeared or been destroyed. For example, as Miguel Leon-Portilla has written of Aztec histories—known as codices—written during and shortly after Cortés's conquest, "The Spanish conquistadors—along with certain churchmen—burned almost all of the codices and destroyed the pre-Hispanic centers of education."[12] To recognize that natives had their own histories and interpretations of events would have called into question the fundamental assumptions of conquest and conversion, which relied on fundamental divisions between European and native.

Exchange Across the Atlantic

Because indigenous voices were frequently distorted or silenced, their perspectives were largely absent from debates and discussions in Europe and have been frequently ignored in histories of the age of exploration. And explorers' firsthand narratives reinforced this, centering on travel from east to west across the Atlantic and the changes wrought in the New World. Focusing on these one-way accounts does not just silence the perspectives of the natives but also downplays other important factors and can lead to the impression that ships, people, products, and ideas traveled in only one direction. Yet in many vital ways, many benefits went from west to east and crossed the Atlantic to affect Europe itself.

In addition to the vast amounts of wealth in gold and silver shipped back to countries such as Spain, and the increasingly developed and coordinated slave trade that at first sent Caribbean island natives to Europe and then began importing Africans to the Americas, many natural products unknown in Europe came back with the returning ships. Such vital staple goods as potatoes, tomatoes, and corn were among these beneficial cargoes brought back to the Old World. Other goods, such as tobacco, cacao, peanuts, avocados, pineapples, and vanilla, were introduced to Europe as well.

On a less tangible but perhaps more important level, the discovery of the Americas brought, for many Europeans, the opportunity to raise and begin to answer questions about their own societies and beliefs. Writers such as French essayist and philosopher Michel de Montaigne, for example, began thinking about the "savages" of the New World in ways that questioned the rightness and legitimacy of many European attitudes. And the very existence of the Americas in many ways signaled that the wisdom of the ancients (such as the Egyptians, Greeks, and Romans)—upon which much of European society was modeled and built—was not infallible and all encompassing, for the ancients had written nothing about the existence of these new lands or the remarkable civilizations there. And as the examples of Bartolomé de Las Casas and others suggest, encounters in these new worlds with such vastly different civilizations and cultures forced into the open important debates about Christianity and the best ways to spread its message.

Remembering the Early Explorers

The practices of the explorers, conquerors, and colonizers in the New World were not universally accepted and admired in Europe. Monarchs such as Isabella and Ferdinand of Spain at times expressed their discomfort with the seizing of Indians as slaves for return to Europe. People such as Las Casas and Cabeza de Vaca condemned the blatant violence against and exploitation of native peoples; their writings demonstrate their own convictions and beliefs and attest to the fact that alternative ways of thinking did in fact exist.

Yet as the firsthand accounts demonstrate, the exploration of the New World was an often incredible undertaking, as not just leaders of expeditions but the sailors, settlers, and soldiers they relied upon at times displayed remarkable courage and endurance. And the inhabitants of these new lands exhibited tremendous curiosity and openness, followed by resourcefulness and resistance. Whether venturing into an unknown sea or interacting with vastly different cultures and peoples, the participants in the age of exploration set in motion forces that introduced two worlds to each other and shaped the world we know today.

Seventeenth-Century North America

By the end of the sixteenth and beginning of the seventeenth centuries, the New World was no longer so new. Although knowledge about the precise geographic boundaries and interiors of the American continents was still very limited, it was becoming clearer that the wonders of these new lands had largely been discovered. For the European, encountering a native or native village was not so strange or exciting as it was for his predecessor. And for many natives, curiosity about these newcomers had turned to suspicion and fear.

Yet the later narratives still retain many of the same elements as those earlier accounts. Representing European voices, they are at a loss to fully depict or comprehend the people and societies they encountered. Although the age of the conquistador was ending, the actions and writings of Spaniard Juan de Oñate, who established the first Spanish settlement in what is now New Mexico, do not seem so far removed from forerunners such as Cortés or Pizarro. Oñate's tale is also one of long and arduous journeys, battles for survival, and exploration of unmapped territories.

Similarly, missionary explorers such as the Frenchman Jacques Marquette, while exhibiting little of the violence of the conquistadors, relied on the same motives of spreading

Christianity and converting the natives that had been appealed to for more than a century in the New World. As with earlier expeditions, Marquette's combined exploration with the missionary impulse, and his accomplishment of navigating almost the entirety of the Mississippi River, also extended previous rivalries between powers of the Old World. With the Spanish moving up into North America from the south, and the English and Dutch establishing colonies on the east, the French were making their way across the Great Lakes region and down the center of the continent. Such expansion depended upon brave explorers making their way through unknown territory, and Marquette's journal draws upon many of the same depictions of heroism as the narratives of the previous centuries of exploration.

With this continuity of the heroic tale for many centuries, it can be easy to overlook the many hidden realities underlying these voyages of exploration and the narratives written about them. It can also be tempting to construct a clear and definite understanding of the lives and times of the explorers and the natives they encountered. Yet this would be to read the stories as simple truths, to forget that their authors had specific goals in mind when writing and utilized specific techniques when constructing their tales. As scholar Stephen Greenblatt suggests, the written narratives of European explorers tell us not so much about what the natives and geography of the New World were "really" like, but they do tell us much about European practices of representation, understanding, and storytelling.

Notes

1. Frederick J. Pohl, *Amerigo Vespucci: Pilot Major.* New York: Octagon Books, 1966, p. 48.

2. Samuel Eliot Morison, *Christopher Columbus, Mariner.* Boston: Little, Brown, 1942, p. 4.

3. Herbert Eugene Bolton, ed., *Spanish Exploration in the Southwest, 1542–1706.* New York: Barnes & Noble, 1963, p. 34.

4. John R. Hale and the Editors of Time-Life Books, *Age of Exploration.* New York: Time, 1966, p. 15.

5. Quoted in Charles L.G. Anderson, *Life and Letters of Vasco Núñez de Balboa*. New York: Fleming H. Revell, 1941, p. 112.

6. Dan O'Sullivan, *The Age of Discovery, 1400–1550*. London: Longman, 1984, p. 18.

7. Quoted in James A. Williamson, *The Cabot Voyages and Bristol Discovery Under Henry VII*. Cambridge, UK: Cambridge University Press, 1962, p. 228.

8. Jim Bailey, *Sailing to Paradise: The Discovery of the Americas by 7000 B.C.* New York: Simon & Schuster, 1994, p. 388.

9. Ross Hassig, "The Collision of Two Worlds," in *The Oxford History of Mexico*, ed. Michael C. Meyer and William H. Beezley. New York: Oxford University Press, 2000, p. 112.

10. Jerald T. Milanich, ed., *The Hernando de Soto Expedition*. New York: Garland, 1991, p. xviii.

11. Bartolomé de Las Casas, *History of the Indies*. Trans. and ed. by Andrée Collard. New York: Harper & Row, 1971, p. 271.

12. Miguel Leon-Portilla, ed., *The Broken Spears: The Aztec Account of the Conquest of Mexico*. Boston: Beacon, 1962, p. xxviii.

Chapter 1

In Search of a
Water Route
to Asia

Chapter Preface

In the late thirteenth century, Italian Marco Polo wrote a book about his travels in Asia. He had traveled there on lengthy overland routes but gained special attention by returning part of the way by sea. In his book, he proclaimed the riches of the "Indies"—a general and vague geographic term encompassing India, China, and countries of the Far East. The well-circulated book played a major role in inspiring European merchants and explorers in later decades to search for a shorter sea route to these lands that produced such an array of luxury goods and spices.

Approximately one hundred years later, a Portuguese prince who came to be known as Henry the Navigator added to the enthusiasm by supporting voyages of discovery and settlement to islands in the Atlantic such as Madeira, the Canaries, and the Azores, which served as important supply stations for journeys across the seas. Henry's zeal for exploration and the spreading of Christianity also resulted in many expeditions down the coast of Africa in search of the water route to the Indian Ocean. This flurry of activity and interest established Portugal as a dominant sea power in the age of exploration.

Explorers by the time of Christopher Columbus could thank such people as Marco Polo and Henry the Navigator for both kindling an interest in exploration and commerce and expanding the boundaries of what was known about the world's geography. Still, though, speculation and theory easily matched factual knowledge about lengthy sea voyages. Explorers in the fifteenth and sixteenth centuries relied on maps and legends that posited the existence of mythical lands, such as Antilia, Hy Brasil, and St. Brendan's Isle—vaguely described islands or mainlands somewhere to the west in the Atlantic. Yet for the voyagers such as Columbus, each new day without sighting any forms of land brought increased anxiety and fear: of winds that blew them across the Atlantic that might not take them back, of running out of supplies, of common sea maladies such as scurvy, or of being lost in storms or wrecked on uncharted rocks or reefs.

Furthermore, many travel narratives available in the fifteenth century contained fantastic descriptions of monstrous races populating the unexplored regions of the globe. For example, *Mandeville's Travels*, taken by some as being based on reality but scoffed at by others as the fiction that it actually was, thrilled readers with stories of headless men with eyes in their shoulders and mouths in their chests. And sometimes, as with the case of the expedition of Ferdinand Magellan, even when land was found and monsters were not, mutinous sailors and officers turned back to the safety of the old country.

Thus, the famous explorers and anonymous sailors of the fifteenth and sixteenth centuries built their accomplishments on the limited knowledge, speculation, and curiosity of their predecessors. They had very specific goals in their endeavors—including the spread of commerce and Christianity. Yet in many respects their information was severely limited, and their journeys across the oceans and around the globe really were voyages into the unknown.

Sailing an Unknown Ocean with an Anxious Crew

Christopher Columbus

Christopher Columbus spent several years trying to get support from various European monarchs for his quest to reach Asia by traveling west across the Atlantic Ocean. Although he confidently asserted that the route must exist, no one was sure if he was right, how long the crossing would be, or whether the seas were even navigable. Columbus obtained Spain's backing and fitted out three ships—the *Nina*, the *Pinta*, and the *Santa Maria*—for a voyage in 1492. Once the trip was underway, the tremendous uncertainties of what lay ahead meant that Columbus had to worry especially about the loyalty of his crew.

In shipboard journal entries, existent only in a paraphrased and heavily edited manuscript by Bartolomé de Las Casas, Columbus gives signs of the great highs and lows he and his crew felt during their thirty-three-day voyage. Captain and crew alike had many questions: Was the distance from the Canary Islands to Japan really twenty-four-hundred nautical miles, as Columbus supposed? (In actuality, the distance is more than four times that length.) If the winds carried them one direction across the ocean, how could the ships sail back to Europe? If the crew realized just how far they were from familiar land after a few weeks, would they force Columbus to return home? These and other questions permeate the selections below, which show how Columbus deceived his

Christopher Columbus, *Journal of First Voyage to America*. New York: Albert and Charles Boni, 1924.

crew in an attempt to make them think they were closer to
Europe than they actually were, how all hands were eager to
turn just about any observation into a sign that land was near
(even as early as nine days into the voyage), and how even
from the beginning, Columbus had reason to suspect that his
men might turn against him.

After finally sighting land, Columbus thought he had succeeded in his quest for a route to the Indies. Although he was
wrong on this count, he had instead achieved something more
momentous: introducing the New World to the old.

The editor of Columbus's journal, Bartolomé de Las Casas,
sailed to the New World in 1502 to oversee land granted to
his father, a crewman who joined Columbus on his second
trip across the Atlantic in 1493.

Friday, Aug. 3d, 1492. Set sail from the bar of Saltes
[north of the Spanish port City of Cadiz] at 8 o'clock,
and proceeded with a strong breeze till sunset, sixty miles
or fifteen leagues S. afterwards S.W. and S. by W. which is
the direction of the Canaries. . . .

Monday, Aug. 6th. The rudder of the caravel Pinta became
loose, being broken or unshipped. It was believed that this
happened by the contrivance of Gomez Rascon and Christopher Quintero, who were on board the caravel, because they
disliked the voyage. The Admiral [Columbus] says he had
found them in an unfavourable disposition before setting out.
He was in much anxiety at not being able to afford any assistance in this case, but says that it somewhat quieted his apprehensions to know that Martin Alonzo Pinzon, Captain of
the Pinta, was a man of courage and capacity. Made a
progress, day and night, of twenty-nine leagues.

Tuesday, Aug. 7th. The Pinta's rudder again broke loose;
secured it, and made for the island of Lanzarote, one of the
Canaries. Sailed, day and night, twenty-five leagues.

Wednesday, Aug. 8th. There were divers opinions among
the pilots of the three vessels, as to their true situation, and
it was found that the Admiral was the most correct. His ob-

ject was to reach the island of Grand Canary, and leave there the Pinta, she being leaky, besides having her rudder out of order, and take another vessel there, if any one could be had. They were unable to reach the island that day.

Thursday, Aug. 9th. The Admiral did not succeed in reaching the island of Gomera [one of the Canary Islands, which also include Teneriffe and Ferro] till Sunday night. Martin Alonzo remained at Grand Canary by command of the Admiral, he being unable to keep the other vessels company. The Admiral afterwards returned to Grand Canary, and there with much labor repaired the Pinta, being assisted by Martin Alonzo and the others; finally they sailed to Gomera. They saw a great eruption of flames from the Peak of Teneriffe; which is a lofty mountain. The Pinta, which before had carried latine sails, they altered and made her square-rigged. Returned to Gomera, Sunday, Sept. 2d, with the Pinta repaired.

Uncharted Waters Ahead

The Admiral says that he was assured by many respectable Spaniards, inhabitants of the island of Ferro . . . that they every year saw land to the west of the Canaries; and others of Gomera affirmed the same with the like assurances. The Admiral here says that he remembers, while he was in Portugal, in 1484, there came a person to the King from the island of Madeira, soliciting for a vessel to go in quest of land, which he affirmed he saw every year, and always of the same appearance. He also says that he remembers the same was said by the inhabitants of the Azores and described as in a similar direction, and of the same shape and size.[1] Having taken in wood, water, meat and other provisions, which had been provided by the men which he left ashore on departing for Grand Canary to repair the Pinta,

1. A meteoric appearance observed to the west of the Canaries occasioned the inhabitants of those islands to imagine they saw a country in that direction. . . . The inhabitants, also, of Madeira and the Azores, deceived by an appearance similar to the above, entertained the belief that land existed to the west of them. This belief was current from the middle of the fifteenth century, and many expeditions were undertaken for the discovery of these countries, some of them by the orders of the King of Portugal. Although they met with no success, the popular imagination of the existence of these territories still continued.

the Admiral took his final departure from Gomera with the three vessels on Thursday, Sept. 6th. . . .

Deceiving the Crew

Sunday, Sept. 9th. Sailed this day nineteen leagues, and determined to count less than the true number, that the crew might not be dismayed if the voyage should prove long. In the night sailed one hundred and twenty miles, at the rate of ten miles an hour, which make thirty leagues. The sailors steered badly, causing the vessels to fall to leeward toward the Northeast, for which the Admiral reprimanded them repeatedly.

Monday, Sept. 10th. This day and night sailed sixty leagues, at the rate of ten miles an hour, which are two leagues and a half. Reckoned only forty-eight leagues, that the men might not be terrified if they should be long upon the voyage.

Tuesday, Sept. 11th. Steered their course W. and sailed above twenty leagues; saw a large fragment of the mast of a vessel, apparently of a hundred and twenty tons, but could not pick it up. In the night sailed about twenty leagues, and reckoned only sixteen, for the cause above stated. . . .

Signs of Land?

Friday, Sept. 14th. Steered this day and night W. twenty leagues; reckoned somewhat less. The crew of the Nina stated that they had seen a *grajao* [sea bird], and a tropic bird, or water-wagtail, which birds never go farther than twenty-five leagues from the land.

Saturday, Sept. 15th. Sailed day and night, W. twenty-seven leagues and more. In the beginning of the night saw a remarkable bolt of fire fall into the sea at the distance of four or five leagues.

Sunday, Sept. 16th. Sailed day and night, W. thirty-nine leagues, and reckoned only thirty-six. Some clouds arose and it drizzled. The Admiral here says that from this time they experienced very pleasant weather, and that the mornings were most delightful, wanting nothing but the melody of the nightingales. He compares the weather to that of Andalusia in April. Here they began to meet with large patches of weeds very green, and which appeared to have been recently washed away from the land; on which account they all judged themselves to be near some island,[2] though not a continent, according to the opinion of the Admiral, who says, *"the continent we shall find further ahead."*

Monday, Sept. 17th. Steered W. and sailed, day and night, above fifty leagues; wrote down only forty-seven; the current favoured them. They saw a great deal of weed which proved to be rock-weed, it came from the W. and they met with it very frequently. They were of opinion that land was near. The pilots took the sun's amplitude, and found that the needles varied to the N.W. a whole point of the compass; the seamen were terrified, and dismayed without saying why. The Admiral discovered the cause, and ordered them to take the amplitude again the next morning, when they found that the needles were true; the cause was that the star moved from its place, while the needles remained stationary.[3] At dawn they saw many more weeds, apparently river weeds, and among them a live crab, which the Admiral kept, and says that these are sure signs of land, being never found eighty leagues out at sea. They found the sea-water less salt since they left the Canaries, and the air more mild. They were all very cheerful, and strove which vessel should outsail the others, and be the first to discover land; they saw many tunnies [tuna], and the crew of the Nina killed one. The Admiral here says that these signs were from the west, "where I hope that high God in whose hand is all victory will speedily direct us to land." This morning he says he saw a white bird called a water-wagtail, or tropic bird, which does not sleep at sea. . . .

The Admiral Worries About His Crew

Saturday, Sept. 22d. Steered about W.N.W. varying their course, and making thirty leagues' progress. Saw few weeds. Some *pardelas* [birds] were seen, and another bird. The Ad-

2. They were, in fact, at this time in the neighborhood of a shoal afterwards discovered.
3. This explanation of the phenomenon was invented by Columbus to quiet the apprehensions of his crews.

miral here says, *"this head wind was very necessary to me, for my crew had grown much alarmed, dreading that they never should meet in these seas with a fair wind to return to Spain."* Part of the day saw no weeds, afterwards great plenty of it.

Sunday, Sept. 23d. Sailed N.W. and N.W. by N. and at times W. nearly twenty-two leagues. Saw a turtle dove, a pelican, a river bird, and other white fowl;—weeds in abundance with crabs among them. The sea being smooth and tranquil, the sailors murmured, saying that they had got into smooth water, where it would never blow to carry them back to Spain; but afterwards the sea rose without wind, which astonished them. The Admiral says on this occasion *"the rising of the sea was very favourable to me, as it happened formerly to Moses when he led the Jews from Egypt."* . . .

Confusion, Disappointment, and Fear

Tuesday, Sept. 25th. Very calm this day; afterwards the wind rose. Continued their course W. till night. The Admiral held a conversation with Martin Alonzo Pinzon, captain of the Pinta, respecting a chart which the Admiral had sent him three days before, in which it appears he had marked down certain islands in that sea; Martin Alonzo was of opinion that they were in their neighbourhood, and the Admiral replied that he thought the same, but as they had not met with them, it must have been owing to the currents which had carried them to the N.E. and that they had not made such progress as the pilots stated. The Admiral directed him to return the chart, when he traced their course upon it in presence of the pilot and sailors.

At sunset Martin Alonzo called out with great joy from his vessel that he saw land, and demanded of the Admiral a reward for his intelligence. The Admiral says, when he heard him declare this, he fell on his knees and returned thanks to God, and Martin Alonzo with his crew repeated *Gloria in excelsis Deo*, as did the crew of the Admiral. Those on board the Nina ascended the rigging, and all declared they saw land. The Admiral also thought it was land, and about twenty-five leagues distant. They remained all night repeating these affirmations, and the Admiral ordered their course to be shifted from W. to S.W. where the land appeared to lie. They sailed that day four leagues and a half W. and in the night seventeen leagues S.W., in all twenty-one and a half: told the crew thirteen leagues, making it a point to keep them from knowing how far they had sailed; in this manner two reckonings were kept, the shorter one falsified, and the other being the true account. The sea was very smooth and many of the sailors went in it to bathe, saw many dories and other fish.

Wednesday, Sept. 26th. Continued their course W. till the afternoon, then S.W. and discovered that what they had taken for land was nothing but clouds. Sailed, day and night, thirty-one leagues; reckoned to the crew twenty-four. The sea was like a river, the air soft and mild. . . .

Monday, Oct. 1st. Continued their course W. and sailed twenty-five leagues; reckoned to the crew twenty. Experienced a heavy shower. The pilot of the Admiral began to fear this morning that they were five hundred and seventy-eight leagues West of the island of Ferro. The short reckoning which the Admiral showed his crew gave five hundred and eighty-four, but the true one which he kept to himself was seven hundred and seven leagues. . . .

Wednesday, Oct. 10th. Steered W.S.W. and sailed at times ten miles an hour, at others twelve, and at others, seven; day and night made fifty-nine leagues' progress; reckoned to the crew but forty-four. Here the men lost all patience, and complained of the length of the voyage, but the Admiral encouraged them in the best manner he could, representing the profits they were about to acquire, and adding that it was to no purpose to complain, having come so far, they had nothing to do but continue on to the Indies, till with the help of our Lord, they should arrive there.

Land at Last!

Thursday, Oct. 11th. Steered W.S.W.; and encountered a heavier sea than they had met with before in the whole voyage. Saw *pardelas* and a green rush near the vessel. The crew of the Pinta saw a cane and a log; they also picked up a stick which appeared to have been carved with an iron tool, a piece of cane, a plant which grows on land, and a board. The crew of the Nina saw other signs of land, and a stalk loaded with roseberries. These signs encouraged them, and they all grew cheerful. Sailed this day till sunset, twenty-seven leagues.

After sunset steered their original course W. and sailed twelve miles an hour till two hours after midnight, going

A Different View of Columbus's Claims to Greatness

Seneca historian John Mohawk provides an important discussion of the ways in which the "heroes" of history are remembered. In the following excerpt, Mohawk argues that Columbus was a remarkable man for a number of reasons, few of which are prevalent in the most common stories told about this explorer.

The legend of Christopher Columbus's "discovery" of the Americas in 1492 is one of the most widely shared stories in the world. Columbus's story has been reinvented, certain specific events have been selected and whole trends of the time have been ignored. The resulting pattern is intended to explain and celebrate the events of the time as part of a glorious history of Western civilization. . . .

We celebrate Columbus (those who do celebrate his achievements) because he found land, but finding land was incidental. . . . What Columbus did that set him apart from the others was to provide the information necessary to make crossing and recrossing the Atlantic possible. . . .

Three things contributed to Columbus's claim to greatness. The first was his astute observation, gained from his voyages to the North Atlantic and the Guinea coast, that the prevailing winds in the north blew east across the Atlantic to Europe and to the south blew west, always west. The second was the fact that European sailing and military technology had advanced far beyond that of any other people in the world and Columbus carried aboard his ships technologies ninety miles, which are twenty-two leagues and a half; and as the Pinta was the swiftest sailer, and kept ahead of the Admiral, she discovered land and made the signals which had been ordered. The land was first seen by a sailor called Rodrigo de Triana, although the Admiral at ten o'clock that evening standing on the quarter-deck saw a light, but so small a body that he could not affirm it to be land; calling to Pero Gutierrez, groom of the King's wardrobe, he told him

---

(including a tradition of literacy which could record his every move) mostly unavailable to his predecessors. The third was the development in Europe at that moment of the commercialization of militarism which made such voyages and the subsequent discoveries not only possible but also compelling in terms of practical conquest. The development of the commercialization of militarism is extremely important and lives with us still. . . .

Western historians would weave a cocoon of mythology around the story of Columbus as had been done with countless other heroic figures, and would in time anoint the story as historical fact. . . .

Can it be that the celebration of Columbus's "discovery," in full view of the historical context, is one of the great propaganda victories of history? The colonization is a story of military conquest carried out by a people possessing vastly superior arms against sometimes practically unarmed populations, of subduing and sometimes exterminating those populations, of appropriating their land and their labor to the ends of the conquerors.

The Doctrine of Discovery, an agreement among the competing military states of Europe, ensured that whichever of them first encountered a place, that power had first rights to explore and colonize that place. It soon became the practice that this "right of discovery" applied whether the place was occupied by people or not. In fact, under such principles the existence of distinct peoples became legally irrelevant.

John Mohawk, "Discovering Columbus: The Way Here," in *Confronting Columbus: An Anthology.* Ed. John Yewell, Chris Dodge, and Jan DeSirey. Jefferson, NC: McFarland, 1992.

he saw a light, and bid him look that way, which he did and saw it; he did the same to Rodrigo Sanchez of Segovia, whom the King and Queen had sent with the squadron as comptroller, but he was unable to see it from his situation. The Admiral again perceived it once or twice, appearing like the light of a wax candle moving up and down, which some thought an indication of land. But the Admiral held it for certain that land was near; for which reason, after they had said the *Salve* which the seamen are accustomed to repeat and chant after their fashion, the Admiral directed them to keep a strict watch upon the forecastle and look out diligently for land, and to him who should first discover it he promised a silken jacket, besides the reward which the King and Queen had offered, which was an annuity of ten thousand maravedis.[4] At two o'clock in the morning the land was discovered, at two leagues' distance; they took in sail and remained under the square-sail lying to till day, which was Friday, when they found themselves near a small island, one of the Lucayos, called in the Indian language Guanahani.[5] Presently they descried people, naked, and the Admiral landed in the boat, which was armed, along with Martin Alonzo Pinzon, and Vincent Yanez his brother, captain of the Nina. The Admiral bore the royal standard, and the two captains each a banner of the Green Cross, which all the ships had carried; this contained the initials of the names of the King and Queen each side of the cross, and a crown over each letter. Arrived on shore, they saw trees very green, many streams of water, and diverse sorts of fruits. The Admiral called upon the two Captains, and the rest of the crew who landed, as also to Rodrigo de Escovedo notary of the fleet, and Rodrigo Sanchez, of Segovia, to bear witness that he before all others took possession (as in fact he did) of that island for the King and Queen his sovereigns, making the requisite declarations, which are more at large set down here in writing.

---

4. The reward for the discovery was adjudged by the King and Queen to be justly due to Columbus, as he was the first who saw the light. The annuity of 10,000 maravedis was therefore punctually paid him through the rest of his life.   5. Historians are not in agreement as to which island Columbus first encountered. They do agree, however, that it was in the group now known as the Bahamas.

Across the North Atlantic

Various Correspondents in England

Merchant and explorer John Cabot was born in Genoa and raised in Venice. He arrived in the port of Bristol, England, around the time that Columbus was making his first voyages. In Bristol, mariners had already been sending out expeditions into the Atlantic, and Cabot convinced England's Henry VII to support a journey across the ocean in search of a route to Cathay (China). His one small ship and crew of twenty made it across the North Atlantic in 1497—a shorter distance to the New World than Columbus's course—and cruised up the coast of Newfoundland for a few weeks before returning to England. This European landing on the North American continent sent shock waves throughout Europe in this age of discovery.

Although no eyewitness accounts of the expedition exist, the letters excerpted below—from a Venetian merchant in London to his brothers, from an unidentified author to the Duke of Milan, from Milan's ambassador in England, from an English merchant and confidant of Columbus, and from an envoy in England to the Spanish crown—illustrate the rivalries between European powers fueled by the quest for routes to Asia and discoveries of new territory. They also depict the difficulties facing leaders and explorers in their search for accurate and current information about geography, climate, and the expeditions of others. Additionally, the Cabot voyage added to the debate about an increasingly important question: To whom did the New World belong?

James A. Williamson, *The Cabot Voyages and Bristol Discovery Under Henry VII*. London: Cambridge University Press, 1962.

Lorenzo Pasqualigo [a Venetian Merchant] to His Brothers at Venice, 23 August 1497

That Venetian of ours who went with a small ship from Bristol to find new islands has come back and says he has discovered mainland 700 leagues away, which is the country of the Grand Khan [supposed ruler of the Far East], and that he coasted it for 300 leagues and landed and did not see any person; but he has brought here to the king certain snares which were spread to take game and a needle for making nets, and he found certain notched [or felled] trees so that by this he judges that there are inhabitants. Being in doubt he returned to his ship; and he has been three months on the voyage; and this is certain. And on the way back he saw two islands, but was unwilling to land, in order not to lose time, as he was in want of provisions. The king [Henry VII] here is much pleased at this; and he [Cabot] says that the tides are slack and do not run as they do here. The king has promised him for the spring ten armed ships as he [Cabot] desires and has given him all the prisoners to be sent away, that they may go with him, as he has requested; and has given him money that he may have a good time until then, and he is with his Venetian wife and his sons at Bristol. His name is Zuam Talbot and he is called the Great Admiral and vast honour is paid to him and he goes dressed in silk, and these English run after him like mad, and indeed he can enlist as many of them as he pleases, and a number of our rogues as well. The discoverer of these things planted on the land which he has found a large cross with a banner of England and one of St Mark, as he is a Venetian, so that our flag has been hoisted very far afield.

News Sent from London to the Duke of Milan, 24 August 1497

News received from England this morning by letters dated the 24th August. . . . Also some months ago his Majesty sent out a Venetian, who is a very good mariner, and has good skill in discovering new islands, and he has returned safe, and has found two very large and fertile new islands. He has also discovered the Seven Cities,[1] 400 leagues from England, on the western passage. This next spring his Majesty means to send him with fifteen or twenty ships. . . .

Raimondo De Raimondi De Soncino [a Milanese Ambassador] to the Duke of Milan, 18 December 1497

Perhaps amid the numerous occupations of your Excellency, it may not weary you to hear how his Majesty [Henry VII] here has gained a part of Asia, without a stroke of the sword. There is in this Kingdom a man of the people, Messer Zoane Caboto [John Cabot] by name, of kindly wit and a most expert mariner. Having observed that the sovereigns first of Portugal and then of Spain had occupied unknown islands, he decided to make a similar acquisition for his Majesty. After obtaining patents that the effective ownership of what he might find should be his, though reserving the rights of the Crown, he committed himself to fortune in a little ship, with eighteen persons. He started from Bristol, a port on the west of this kingdom, passed Ireland, which is still further west, and then bore towards the north, in order to sail to the east, leaving the north on his right hand after some days. After having wandered for some time he at length arrived at the mainland,where he hoisted the royal standard, and took possession for the king here; and after taking certain tokens he returned.

This Messer Zoane, as a foreigner and a poor man, would not have obtained credence, had it not been that his companions, who are practically all English and from Bristol, testified that he spoke the truth. This Messer Zoane has the description of the world in a map, and also in a solid sphere, which he has made, and shows where he has been . . . They say that the land is excellent and temperate, and they believe that Brazil wood [a source of red dye] and silk are native there. They assert that the sea there is swarming with fish,

1. The mythical island of the Seven Cities was thought to have been colonized by Christians fleeing an invasion of Muslims in the eighth century.

which can be taken not only with the net, but in baskets let down with a stone, so that it sinks in the water. I have heard this Messer Zoane state so much.

These same English, his companions, say that they could bring so many fish that this kingdom would have no further need of Iceland, from which place there comes a very great quantity of the fish called stockfish. But Messer Zoane has his mind set upon even greater things, because he proposes to keep along the coast from the place at which he touched, more and more towards the east, until he reaches an island which he calls Cipango [Japan], situated in the equinoctial region, where he believes that all the spices of the world have their origin, as well as the jewels. He says that on previous occasions he has been to Mecca, whither spices are

Searching for a route to China, Cabot sailed across the Atlantic in 1497. The result was the European discovery of Newfoundland.

borne by caravans from distant countries. When he asked those who brought them what was the place of origin of these spices, they answered that they did not know, but that other caravans came with this merchandise to their homes from distant countries, and these again said that the goods had been brought to them from other remote regions. He therefore reasons that these things come from places far away from them, and so on from one to the other, always assuming that the earth is round, it follows as a matter of course that the last of all must take them in the north towards the west.

He tells all this in such a way, and makes everything so plain, that I also feel compelled to believe him. What is much more, his Majesty, who is wise and not prodigal, also gives him some credence, because he is giving him a fairly good provision, since his return, so Messer Zoane himself tells me. Before very long they say that his Majesty will equip some ships, and in addition he will give them all the malefactors, and they will go to that country and form a colony. By means of this they hope to make London a more important mart for spices than Alexandria. . . .

I have also spoken with a Burgundian, one of Messer Zoane's companions, who corroborates everything. He wants to go back, because the Admiral, which is the name they give to Messer Zoane, has given him an island. He has given another to his barber, a Genoese by birth, and both consider themselves counts, while my lord the Admiral esteems himself at least a prince.

I also believe that some poor Italian friars will go on this voyage, who have the promise of bishoprics. As I have made friends with the Admiral, I might have an archbishopric if I chose to go there, but I have reflected that the benefices which your Excellency reserves for me are safer, and I therefore beg that possession may be given me of those which fall vacant in my absence, and the necessary steps taken so that they may not be taken away from me by others, who have the advantage of being on the spot. Meanwhile I stay on in this country, eating ten or twelve courses at each meal, and spending three hours at table twice every day, for the love of your Excellency, to whom I humbly commend myself.

John Day [an English Merchant] to the Lord Grand Admiral

Your Lordship's servant brought me your letter. I have seen its contents and I would be most desirous and most happy to serve you. . . . I am sending the other book of Marco Polo and a copy of the land which has been found. I do not send the map because I am not satisfied with it; . . . but from the said copy your Lordship will learn what you wish to know, for in it are named the capes of the mainland and the islands, and thus you will see where land was first sighted, since most of the land was discovered after turning back. Thus your Lordship will know that the cape nearest to Ireland is 1800 miles west of Dursey Head which is in Ireland, and the southernmost part of the Island of the Seven Cities is west of Bordeaux River, and your Lordship will know that he [Cabot] landed at only one spot of the mainland, near the place where land was first sighted, and they disembarked there with a crucifix and raised banners with the arms of the Holy Father and those of the King of England, my master; and they found tall trees of the kind masts are made, and other smaller trees, and the country is very rich in grass. In that particular spot, as I told your Lordship, they found a trail that went inland, they saw a site where a fire had been made, they saw manure of animals which they thought to be farm animals, and they saw a stick half a yard long pierced at both ends, carved and painted with brazil, and by such signs they believe the land to be inhabited. Since he was with just a few people, he did not dare advance inland beyond the shooting distance of a cross-bow. . . .

Following the shore they saw two forms running on land one after the other, but they could not tell if they were human beings or animals; and it seemed to them that there were fields where they thought might also be villages, and they saw a forest whose foliage looked beautiful.

They left England toward the end of May, and must have been on the way 35 days before sighting land; the wind was east-north-east and the sea calm going and coming back, except for one day when he ran into a storm two or three days before finding land; and going so far out, his compass needle failed to point north and marked two rhumbs [points on the compass] below. They spent about one month discovering the coast and from the above mentioned cape of the mainland which is nearest to Ireland, they returned to the coast of Europe in fifteen days. They had the wind behind them, and he reached Brittany because the sailors confused him, saying that he was heading too far north. From there he came to Bristol, and he went to see the King to report to him all the above mentioned; and the King granted him an annual pension of twenty pounds sterling to sustain himself until the time comes when more will be known of this business, since with God's help it is hoped to push through plans for exploring the said land more thoroughly next year with ten or twelve vessels—because in his voyage he had only one ship of fifty 'toneles' and twenty men and food for seven or eight months—and they want to carry out this new project. . . .

Rest assured, Magnificent Lord, of my desire and natural intention to serve you . . . , and when I get news from England about the matters referred to above—for I am sure that everything has to come to my knowledge—I will inform your Lordship of all that would not be prejudicial to the King my master. In payment for some services which I hope to render you, I beg your Lordship to kindly write me about such matters, because the favour you will thus do me will greatly stimulate my memory to serve you in all the things that may come to my knowledge.

Pedro De Ayala [a Spanish Envoy] to the Spanish Sovereigns, 25 July 1498

I think Your Highnesses have already heard how the king of England has equipped a fleet to explore certain islands or mainland which he has been assured certain persons who set out last year from Bristol in search of the same have discovered. I have seen the map made by the discoverer, who is another Genoese like Columbus, who has been in Seville and at Lisbon seeking to obtain persons to aid him in this discovery. For the last seven years the people of Bristol have equipped two, three [and] four caravels to go in search of the island of Brazil[2] and the Seven Cities according to the fancy of this Genoese. The king made up his mind to send thither, because last year sure proof was brought him they had found land. The fleet he prepared, which consisted of five vessels, was provisioned for a year. News has come that one of these . . . has made land in Ireland in a great storm with the ship badly damaged. The Genoese kept on his way. Having seen the course they are steering and the length of the voyage, I find that what they have discovered or are in search of is possessed by Your Highnesses because it is at the cape which fell to Your Highnesses by the convention with Portugal.[3] It is hoped they will be back by September. I let [? will let] Your Highnesses know about it. The king has spoken to me several times on the subject. He hopes the affair may turn out profitable. I believe the distance is not 400 leagues. I told him that I believed the islands were those found by Your Highnesses, and although I gave him the main reason, he would not have it. Since I believe Your Highnesses will already have notice of all this and also of the chart or mappemonde which this man has made, I do not send it now, although it is here, and so far as I can see exceedingly false, in order to make believe that these are not part of the said islands.

2. An island in the Atlantic supposedly visited previously by mariners from Bristol.
3. The 1494 Treaty of Tordesillas, which stated that all new lands discovered west of a certain line would belong to Spain and lands east would be Portugal's. Despite the agreement, dividing up the New World would still be a source of contention among European powers for many years.

Finding the Straits of Magellan

Antonio Pigafetta

Although Amerigo Vespucci's discoveries had suggested otherwise, explorers such as Christopher Columbus and Ferdinand Magellan still believed that the landmass of South America was actually just an extension of the Asian continent. In 1519, Magellan, a Portuguese navigator, organized an expedition sponsored by Spain that included five ships and more than two hundred men. The stated destination was the Molucca (Spice) Islands (in present-day Indonesia), and Magellan expected that once he found a way to cut through the Americas, the Moluccas would not be far to the west. He found his passage much farther south than expected, and only after many difficult months of cruising the South American coast and exploring numerous inlets and bays.

The following passages are written by Antonio Pigafetta, an Italian nobleman who accompanied Magellan and was one of approximately thirty men to safely complete the journey not only through the straits but ultimately around the world. Based on the daily notes Pigafetta took during the trip, the record describes the incredible people encountered in South America, Magellan's struggles against mutineers, the momentous discovery of and passage through this uncharted strait, and the terrible hardships faced crossing the unexpectedly vast Pacific—such as, according to Pigafetta, going more than three months without replenishing food and water supplies.

Although Magellan died after making it as far as the Philippines, the fleet continued and one ship—after nearly

Antonio Pigafetta, Maximilian of Transylvania, and Gaspar Corrêa, *Magellan's Voyage Around the World: Three Contemporary Accounts*, edited by Charles E. Nowell. Evanston, IL: Northwestern University Press, 1962.

three years—successfully completed the first circumnaviga-
tion of the globe. Magellan's successes were monumental: he
found the strait that Vespucci (and so many others) had
searched for, demonstrated that the Earth is composed mostly
of water and not land, and proved that the Americas were distinct continents thousands of miles from Asia.

At midnight of Monday, October three [1519], the sails
were trimmed toward the south, and we took to the
open Ocean Sea [leaving from the Canary Islands, off the
northwest coast of Africa], passing between Cape Verde and
its islands in 14 and one-half degrees. Thus for many days
did we sail along the coast of Ghinea, or Ethiopia, where
there is a mountain called Siera Leona, which lies in 8 degrees of latitude, with contrary winds, calms, and rains without wind, until we reached the equinoctial line, having sixty
days of continual rain. Contrary to the opinion of the ancients, before we reached the line many furious squalls of
wind, and currents of water struck us head on in 14 degrees.
As we could not advance, and in order that the ships might
not be wrecked, all the sails were struck; and in this manner
did we wander hither and yon on the sea, waiting for the
tempest to cease, for it was very furious. When it rained
there was no wind. When the sun shone, it was calm. Certain large fishes called *tiburoni* [sharks] came to the side of
the ships. They have terrible teeth, and whenever they find
men in the sea they devour them. We caught many of them
with iron hooks, although they are not good to eat unless
they are small, and even then they are not very good. During those storms the holy body, that is to say St. Elmo, appeared to us many times, in light—among other times on an
exceedingly dark night, with the brightness of a blazing
torch, on the maintop, where he stayed for about two hours
or more, to our consolation, for we were weeping. When
that blessed light was about to leave us, so dazzling was the
brightness that it cast into our eyes, that we all remained for
more than an eighth of an hour blinded and calling for

mercy.[1] And truly when we thought that we were dead men, the sea suddenly grew calm. . . .

Arrival in Brazil

After we had passed the equinoctial line going south, we lost the north star, and hence we sailed south south-west until [we reached] a land called the land of Verzin [Brazil] which lies in 23½ degrees of the Antarctic Pole [south latitude]. It is the land extending from the cape of Santo Augustino, which lies in 8 degrees of the same pole. There we got [from the natives] a plentiful refreshment of fowls, potatoes, many sweet pine-apples—in truth the most delicious fruit that can be found—the flesh of the *anta* [tapir], which resembles beef, sugarcane, and innumerable other things, which I shall not mention in order not to be prolix. For one fishhook or one knife, those people gave 5 or 6 chickens; for one comb, a brace of geese; for one mirror or one pair of scissors, as many fish as would be sufficient for X men; for a bell or one leather lace, one basketful of potatoes. These potatoes resemble chestnuts in taste, and are as long as turnips. For a king of diamonds which is a playing card, they gave me 6 fowls and thought that they had even cheated me. . . .

We finally reached 49 and one-half degrees toward the Antarctic Pole [near the southern-most part of modern-day Argentina]. As it was winter, the ships entered a safe port to winter. We passed two months in that place without seeing anyone. One day we suddenly saw a naked man of giant stature on the shore of the port, dancing, singing, and throwing dust on his head. The captain-general sent one of our men to the giant so that he might perform the same actions as a sign of peace. Having done that, the man led the giant to an islet into the presence of the captain-general. When the giant was in the captain-general's and our presence, he marveled greatly, and made signs with one finger raised upward, believing that we had come from the sky. He was so tall that

---

1. St. Elmo's fire is electricity in the atmosphere that appears in star-shaped form near the masthead of a ship. Other names for it are St. Peter, St. Nicholas, Santa Clara, and Castor and Pollux.

we reached only to his waist, and he was well proportioned. His face was large and painted red all over, while about his eyes he was painted yellow; and he had two hearts painted on the middle of his cheeks. His scanty hair was painted white. He was dressed in the skins of animals skilfully sewn together. That animal has a head and ears as large as those of a mule, a neck and body like those of a camel, the legs of a deer, and the tail of a horse, like which it neighs, and that land has very many of them. His feet were shod with the same kind of skins which covered his feet in the manner of shoes. In his hand he carried a short, heavy bow, with a cord somewhat thicker than those of the lute, and made from the intestines of the same animal, and a bundle of rather short cane arrows feathered like ours, and with points of white and black flint stones in the manner of Turkish arrows, instead of iron. Those points were fashioned by means of another stone. The captain-general had the giant given something to eat and drink, and among other things which were shown to him was a large steel mirror. When he saw his face, he was greatly terrified, and jumped back throwing three or four of our men to the ground. After that he was given some bells, a mirrow, a comb, and certain Pater Nosters. The captain-general sent him ashore with 4 armed men. When one of his companions, who would never come to the ships, saw him coming with our men, he ran to the place where the others were, who came [down to the shore] all naked one after the other. When our men reached them, they began to dance and to sing, lifting one finger to the sky. . . .

Mutiny!

In that port which we called the port of Santo Julianno, we remained about five months. Many things happened there. . . . As soon as we had entered the port, the captains of the other four ships plotted treason in order that they might kill the captain-general. Those conspirators consisted of the overseer of the fleet, one Johan de Cartagena, the treasurer, Alouise de Mendosa, the accountant, Anthonio Cocha, and Gaspar de Cazada. The overseer of the men having been quartered, the treasurer was killed by dagger blows, for the treason was discovered. Some days after that, Gaspar de Cazada, was banished with a priest in that land of Patagonia. The captain-general did not wish to have him killed, because the emperor, Don Carlo, had appointed him captain. A ship called "Sancto Jacobo" was wrecked in an expedition made to explore the coast. All the men were saved as by a miracle, not even getting wet. Two of them came to the ships after suffering great hardships, and reported the whole occurrence to us. . . .

Leaving that place, we found, in 51 degrees less one-third degree, toward the Antarctic Pole, a river of fresh water. There the ships almost perished because of the furious winds; but God and the holy bodies aided them. We stayed about two months in that river in order to supply the ships with water, wood, and fish. . . .

Magellan Discovers a Strait

Then going to fifty-two degrees toward the same pole, we found a strait on the day of the [Feast of the] Eleven Thousand Virgins [October 21], whose head is called Capo de le Undici Millia Vergine because of that very great miracle. That strait is one hundred and ten leguas or 440 miles long, and it is one-half legua broad, more or less. It leads to another sea called the Pacific Sea, and is surrounded by very lofty mountains laden with snow. There it was impossible to find bottom [for anchoring], but [it was necessary to fasten] the moorings on land 25 or 30 brazas away. Had it not been for the captain-general, we would not have found that strait, for we all thought and said that it was closed on all sides. But the captain-general who knew where to sail to find a well-hidden strait, which he saw depicted on a map in the treasury of the king of Portugal, which was made by that excellent man, Martin de Boemia, sent two ships, the "Santo Anthonio" and the "Conceptione" (for thus they were called), to discover what was inside the cape de la Baia. We with the other two ships, the flagship, called "Trinitade," and the other the "Victoria," stayed inside the bay to await them. A great storm struck us that night, which lasted until the middle of next day, which necessitated our lifting anchor, and letting ourselves drift hither and thither about the bay. The other two ships suffered a headwind and could not double a cape formed by the bay almost at its end, as they were trying to return to join us; so that they thought that they would have to run aground. But on approaching the end of the bay, and thinking that they were lost, they saw a small opening which did not appear to be an opening, but a sharp turn. Like desperate men they hauled into it, and thus they discovered the strait by chance. Seeing that it was not a sharp turn, but a strait with land, they proceeded farther, and found a bay. And then farther on they found another strait and another bay larger than the first two. Very joyful they immediately turned back to inform the captain-general. We thought that they had been wrecked, first, by reason of the violent storm, and second, because two days had passed and they had not appeared, and also because of certain [signals with] smoke made by two of their men who had been sent ashore to advise us. And so, while in suspense, we saw the two ships with sails full and banners flying to the wind, coming toward us. When they neared us in this manner, they suddenly discharged a number of mortars, and burst into cheers. Then all together thanking God and the Virgin Mary, we went to seek [the strait] farther on.

A Ship Deserts

After entering that strait, we found two openings, one to the southeast, and the other to the southwest. The captain-general sent the ship "Sancto Anthonio" together with the "Conceptione" to ascertain whether that opening which was toward the southeast had an exit into the Pacific Sea. The ship "Sancto Anthonio" would not await the "Conceptione," because it intended to flee and return to Spagnia—which it did. The pilot of that ship was one Stefan Gomes, and he hated the captain-general exceedingly, because before that fleet was fitted out, the emperor had ordered that he be given some caravels with which to discover lands, but his Majesty did not give them to him because of the coming of the captain-general. On that account he conspired with certain Spaniards, and next night they captured the captain of their ship, a cousin of the captain-general, one Alvaro de Meschita, whom they wounded and put in irons, and in this condition took to Spagnia. The other giant whom we had captured was in that ship, but he died when the heat came on. The "Conceptione," as it could not follow that ship, waited for it, sailing about hither and thither. The "Sancto Anthonio" turned back at night and fled along the same strait. . . .

Through to the Pacific

We had gone to explore the other opening toward the southwest. Finding, however, the same strait continuously, we came upon a river which we called the river of Sardine, because there were many sardines near it. So we stayed there for four days in order to await the two ships. During that period we sent a well-equipped boat to explore the cape of the other sea. The men returned within three days, and reported that they had seen the cape and the open sea. The captain-general wept for joy, and called that cape, Cape Dezeado, for we had been desiring it for a long time. . . .

Had we not discovered that strait, the captain-general had determined to go as far as seventy-five degrees toward the Antarctic Pole. There in that latitude, during the summer season, there is no night, or if there is any night it is but short, and so in the winter with the day. . . . When we were in that strait, the nights were only three hours long, and it was then the month of October. The land on the left-hand side of that strait turned toward the southeast and was low. We called that strait the strait of Patagonia. One finds the safest of ports every half legua in it, water, the finest of wood [but not of cedar], fish, sardines, and *missiglioni* [a type of shellfish], while smallage, a sweet herb [although there is also some that is bitter] grows around the springs. We ate of it for many days as we had nothing else. I believe that there is not a more beautiful or better strait in the world than that one. . . .

Vast Ocean, Terrible Hardship

Wednesday, November 28, 1520, we debouched from that strait, engulfing ourselves in the Pacific Sea. We were three months and twenty days without getting any kind of fresh food. We ate biscuit, which was no longer biscuit, but powder of biscuits swarming with worms, for they had eaten the good. It stank strongly of the urine of rats. We drank yellow water that had been putrid for many days. We also ate some ox hides that covered the top of the mainyard to prevent the yard from chafing the shrouds, and which had become exceedingly hard because of the sun, rain, and wind. We left them in the sea for four or five days, and then placed them for a few moments on top of the embers, and so ate them; and often we ate sawdust from boards. Rats were sold for one-half ducado apiece, and even we could not get them. But above all the other misfortunes the following was the worst. The gums of both the lower and upper teeth of some of our men swelled, so that they could not eat under any circumstances and therefore died.[2] Nineteen men died from that sickness, and the giant together with an Indian from the country of Verzin. Twenty-five or thirty men fell sick [during that time], in the arms, legs, or in another place, so that but few remained well. However, I by the grace of God, suffered no sickness. . . . Had not God and His blessed mother given us so good weather we would all have died of hunger in that exceeding vast sea. Of a verity I believe no such voyage will ever be made [again].

---

2. These are well-known results of scurvy.

A World Unknown to the Ancients

Giovanni da Verrazzano

Giovanni da Verrazzano was an Italian who sailed in the service of France in 1524. Verrazzano's voyage was largely backed by Florentine merchants and bankers in France, and its stated goal was to reach Asia by finding a northern strait through the Americas. Of course, no such strait existed, but in his search Verrazzano ended up charting the coast of North America from approximately South Carolina to Nova Scotia. He landed several times to explore the New World and meet its inhabitants.

In the following account, taken from a report written to King Francis I, Verrazzano, unlike many other explorers, acknowledges that any certain knowledge of the natives he encountered is impossible because of language barriers. While he does not fully recognize their humanity, he does observe that each group he meets is discrete and unique. His observations about geography at times rely on traditional and erroneous assumptions, which, for example, lead him to conclude that one section of the coast he explored was really a narrow isthmus with the "eastern sea" leading to Asia on the other side. But other times, he demonstrates an important awareness that the Old World understanding of what lies across the Atlantic Ocean must be revised. According to Verrazzano, the cosmology presumed by the Ancient Greeks and other Classical civilizations is probably faulty since the land and people he encountered were surely never known to the Ancients.

Lawrence C. Wroth, *The Voyages of Giovanni da Verrazzano, 1524–1528.* New Haven, CT: Yale University Press, 1970. Copyright © 1970 by the Pierpont Morgan Library. Reproduced by permission.

We set sail with the *Dauphine* from the deserted rock near the Island of Madeira, which belongs to the Most Serene King of Portugal, on the 17th day of January last [1524]; we had fifty men, and were provided with food for eight months, with arms and other articles of war, and naval munitions; we sailed westward on the gentle breath of a light easterly wind. In twenty-five days we covered eight hundred leagues. On the 24th day of February we went through a storm as violent as ever sailing man encountered. We were delivered from it with the divine help and goodness of the ship, whose glorious name and happy destiny enabled her to endure the violent waves of the sea. We continued on our westerly course, keeping rather to the north. In another twenty-five days we sailed more than four hundred leagues, where there appeared a new land which had never been seen before by any man, either ancient or modern. At first it appeared to be rather low-lying; having approached to within a quarter of a league, we realized that it was inhabited, for huge fires had been built on the seashore. We saw that the land stretched southward, and coasted along it in search of some port where we might anchor the ship and investigate the nature of the land, but in fifty leagues we found no harbor or place where we could stop with the ship. Seeing that the land continued to the south [*so as not to meet with the Spaniards*],[1] we decided to turn and skirt it toward the north, where we found the land we had sighted earlier. . . .

A Place Unknown

I will now . . . describe the situation and nature of this land. The seashore is completely covered with fine sand fifteen feet deep, which rises in the form of small hills about fifty paces wide. After climbing farther, we found other streams and inlets from the sea which come in by several mouths, and follow the ins and outs of the shoreline. Nearby we could see a stretch of country much higher than the sandy

---

1. Italicized text indicates annotations added to the original manuscript, presumably by Verrazzano himself.

shore, with many beautiful fields and plains full of great
forests, some sparse and some dense; and the trees have so
many colors, and are so beautiful and delightful that they
defy description. And do not think, Your Majesty, that these
forests are like the Hyrcanian Forest or the wild wastelands
of Scythia and the northern countries, full of common trees;
they are adorned and clothed with palms, laurel, cypress,
and other varieties of tree unknown in our Europe. And
these trees emit a sweet fragrance over a large area, the nature of which we could not examine for the reason stated
above, not because we found it difficult to get through the
forests—indeed, they are nowhere so dense as to be impen-
etrable. We think that they belong to the Orient by virtue of
the surroundings, and that they are not without some kind
of narcotic or aromatic liquor. There are other riches, like
gold, which ground of such a color usually denotes. There
is an abundance of animals, stags, deer, hares; and also of
lakes and pools of running water with various types of bird,
perfect for all the delights and pleasures of the hunt. . . .

A Magnificent Deed

We saw many people on the beach making various friendly
signs, and beckoning us ashore; and there I saw a magnificent deed, as Your Majesty will hear. We sent one of our
young sailors swimming ashore to take the people some
trinkets, such as little bells, mirrors, and other trifles, and
when he came within four fathoms of them, he threw them
the goods and tried to turn back, but he was so tossed about
by the waves that he was carried up onto the beach half
dead. Seeing this, the native people immediately ran up;
they took him by the head, the legs, and arms and carried
him some distance away. Whereupon the youth, realizing he
was being carried away like this, was seized with terror, and
began to utter loud cries. They answered him in their language to show him he should not be afraid. Then they
placed him on the ground in the sun, at the foot of a small
hill, and made gestures of great admiration, looking at the
whiteness of his flesh and examining him from head to foot.

They took off his shirt and shoes and hose, leaving him naked, then made a huge fire next to him, placing him near the heat. When the sailors in the boat saw this, they were filled with terror, as always when something new occurs, and thought the people wanted to roast him for food. After remaining with them for a while, he regained his strength, and showed them by signs that he wanted to return to the ship. With the greatest kindness, they accompanied him to the sea, holding him close and embracing him; and then to reassure him, they withdrew to a high hill and stood watching him until he was in the boat. The youth learned the following about these people: they are dark in color like the other [tribes], their skin is very glossy, they are of medium height, their faces are more clear-cut, their body and other limbs much more delicate and much less powerful, but they are more quick-witted. He saw nothing else.

The Eastern Sea

We left this place [*We called it "Annunciata" from the day of arrival, and found there an isthmus one mile wide and about two hundred miles long, in which we could see the eastern sea from the ship, halfway between west and north. This is doubtless the one which goes around the tip of India, China, and Cathay. We sailed along this isthmus, hoping all the time to find some strait or real promontory where the land might end to the north, and we could reach those blessed shores of Cathay. This isthmus was named by the discoverer "Varazanio," just as all the land we found was called "Francesca" after our Francis.*], still following the coast which veered somewhat to the north, and after fifty leagues we reached another land which seemed much more beautiful and full of great forests. . . .

As the Orientals Do

We discovered a triangular-shaped island, ten leagues from the mainland, similar in size to the island of Rhodes; it was full of hills, covered in trees, and highly populated to judge by the fires we saw burning continually along the shore. We baptized it in the name of your illustrious mother, but did not anchor there because the weather was unfavorable. We reached another land fifteen leagues from the island, where we found an excellent harbor; before entering it, we saw about twenty boats full of people who came around the ship uttering various cries of wonderment. They did not come nearer than fifty paces, but stopped to look at the structure of our ship, our persons, and our clothes; then all together they raised a loud cry which meant that they were joyful. We reassured them somewhat by imitating their gestures, and they came near enough for us to throw them a few little bells and mirrors and many trinkets, which they took and looked at, laughing, and then they confidently came on board ship. Among them were two kings, who were as beautiful of stature and build as I can possibly describe. The first was about forty years old, the other a young man of twenty-four, and they were dressed thus: the older man had on his naked body a stag skin, skillfully worked like damask with various embroideries; the head was bare, the hair tied back with various bands, and around the neck hung a wide chain decorated with many different-colored stones. The young man was dressed in almost the same way. These people are the most beautiful and have the most civil customs that we have found on this voyage. They are taller than we are; they are a bronze color, some tending more toward whiteness, others to a tawny color; the face is clear-cut; the hair is long and black, and they take great pains to decorate it; the eyes are black and alert, and their manner is sweet and gentle, very like the manner of the ancients. . . .

Some [of the women] have other hair arrangements such as the women of Egypt and Syria wear, and these women are older and have been joined in wedlock. Both men and women have various trinkets hanging from their ears as the Orientals do; and we saw that they had many sheets of worked copper which they prize more than gold. They do not value gold because of its color; they think it the most worthless of all, and rate blue and red above all other colors. The things we gave them that they prized the most were little bells, blue crystals, and other trinkets to put in the ear or around the neck. They did not appreciate cloth of silk and gold, nor even of any other kind, nor did they care to have them; the same was true for metals like steel and iron, for many times when we showed them some of our arms, they did not admire them, nor ask for them, but merely examined the workmanship. They did the same with mirrors; they would look at them quickly, and then refuse them, laughing. They are very generous and give away all they have. We made great friends with them. . . .

Before Columbus

Historians have long debated the merits of theories and evidence that point to the "discovery" of the New World continents by explorers long before 1492. Claims have been made that voyages from a variety of places took place in the fifteenth century prior to the landmark journey of Christopher Columbus. And evidence has been discovered demonstrating the presence of Norse settlements in North America as early as the tenth century.

Further, as the following passages from historian Samuel D. Marble's book Before Columbus *suggest, exploration across the Atlantic prior to Columbus was likely not limited to Europeans, but came from Africa as well.*

Among those who wondered whether Columbus was the first person to discover the new world was the man Columbus. He recorded in his journal a visit with King Juan of Portugal, who told him before his departure that he, the King, had evidence of trade between Africa and South America in tobacco, cotton, shell money, and bread root for a considerable time in the unknowable past. . . .

As a subject for research, the possibility of African discovery of America has never been a tempting one for American historians. In a sense, we choose our own history, or more accurately, we select those vistas of history for our examinations which promise us the greatest satisfaction, and we have had little appetite to explore the possibility that our founding father was a black man for whom two continents

Brute Creatures

Having supplied all our needs, we left this port on the sixth day of May and continued along the coast, never losing sight of land. We sailed one hundred and fifty leagues and found the land similar in nature, but somewhat higher, with several mountains which all showed signs of minerals. We did not land there because the weather was favorable and helped us in sailing along the coast: we think it resembles the other. The shore ran eastward. At a distance of fifty leagues, keep-

should be named, as well as great nations, rivers and cities. In spite of the remarkable collection of clues assembled by no less a person than Columbus that other sailors had preceded him to America, and that an extensive commerce of African manufacture had been carried on for years through well-defined channels, this chapter of American history has proportionately gone unnoticed and unexplored. And not this chapter alone. In general, the view that the American continents had been explored before 1492 is not one that evokes Yankee enthusiasm. Neither is the possibility that America had been settled by Vikings for five hundred years before the arrival of the little Spanish fleet. Here the motivation was curiosity on the part of the Scandinavians. It was they who found the time to dust off the records and reconcile them with the sagas. It was the descendants of the Vikings who provided labor to dig out stones of an original settlement on the banks of North America. Over the span of years, the Scandinavian evidence became so overwhelming that the defensive historian, Admiral Samuel Eliot Morison, found it necessary to concede that the Greenlanders did precede Columbus to these shores by half a millennium. It was a reluctant conversion but it was an honest one. However, the search of the North European anthropologists for evidence of settlements has only started. More is to come.

Samuel D. Marble, *Before Columbus: The New History of Celtic, Phoenician, Viking, Black African, and Asian Contacts and Impacts in the Americas Before 1492.* New York: A.S. Barnes, 1980.

ing more to the north, we found high country full of very dense forests, composed of pines, cypresses, and similar trees which grow in cold regions. The people were quite different from the others, for while the previous ones had been courteous in manner, these were full of crudity and vices, and were so barbarous that we could never make any communication with them, however many signs we made to them. They were clothed in skins of bear, lynx, sea-wolf and other animals. As far as we could judge from several visits to their houses, we think they live on game, fish, and several fruits which are a species of root which the earth produces itself. They have no pulse [a plant producing edible seeds], and we saw no sign of cultivation, nor would the land be suitable for producing any fruit or grain on account of its sterility. If we wanted to trade with them for some of their things, they would come to the seashore on some rocks where the breakers were most violent, while we remained in the little boat, and they sent us what they wanted to give on a rope, continually shouting to us not to approach the land; they gave us the barter quickly, and would take in exchange only knives, hooks for fishing, and sharp metal. We found no courtesy in them, and when we had nothing more to exchange and left them, the men made all the signs of scorn and shame that any brute creature would make. . . .

Lack of a Common Language

After sailing one hundred fifty leagues in a northeasterly direction we approached the land which the Britons once found, which lies in 50 degrees; and since we had exhausted all our naval stores and provisions, and had discovered seven hundred leagues or more of new land, we took on supplies of water and wood, and decided to return to France. Due to the lack of [a common] language, we were unable to find out by signs or gestures how much religious faith these people we found possess. We think they have neither religion nor laws, that they do not know of a First Cause or Author, that they do not worship the sky, the stars, the sun, the moon, or other planets, nor do they even practice any kind of idolatry; we do not know whether they offer any sacrifices or other prayers, nor are there any temples or churches of prayer among their peoples. We consider that they have no religion and that they live in absolute freedom, and that everything they do proceeds from Ignorance; for they are very easily persuaded, and they imitated everything that they saw us Christians do with regard to divine worship, with the same fervor and enthusiasm that we had.

It remains for me to tell Your Majesty of the progress of this voyage as regards Cosmography. As I said earlier, we departed from the aforementioned rocks which lie at the limit of the Occident as the ancients knew it. . . .

A World Unknown to the Ancients

My intention on this voyage was to reach Cathay and the extreme eastern coast of Asia, but I did not expect to find such an obstacle of new land as I have found; and if for some reason I did expect to find it, I estimated there would be some strait to get through to the Eastern Ocean. This was the opinion of all the ancients, who certainly believed that our Western Ocean was joined to the Eastern Ocean of India without any land in between. Aristotle supports this theory by arguments of various analogies, but this opinion is quite contrary to that of the moderns, and has been proven false by experience. Nevertheless, land has been found by modern man which was unknown to the ancients, another world with respect to the one they knew, which appears to be larger than our Europe, than Africa, and almost larger than Asia, if we estimate its size correctly. . . .

And if the territorial area of this [new] land corresponds in size to its maritime shore, there is no doubt that it is larger than Asia. In this way we find that the extension of the land is much greater than the ancients believed, and contrary to the Mathematicians who considered that there was less land than water, we have proven it by experience to be the reverse.

At the Mercy of the Winds

Juan Rodríguez Cabrillo

Historians have claimed Juan Rodríguez Cabrillo as both
Spanish and Portuguese. They are certain, however, that he
was in the New World by 1510 and participated in the conquest of Cuba and the siege of Tenochtitlán in Mexico with
Hernán Cortés. Because of these and other expeditions,
Cabrillo like many others earned his fortune through
conquest.

In 1542 he took charge of an expedition leaving from the
west coast of Mexico and followed the dangerous and
uncharted coast northward. Like many others, he believed
that America was joined to Asia or separated by a small strait.
He thought that following the California coast northward
would thus open up a route to China. The expedition lasted
more than nine months, faced grave dangers from the elements, and most likely made it as far as present-day Oregon,
but Cabrillo did not survive the trip.

The source of the following account is not entirely certain;
it appears to be based on a log of the journey. This log, kept
by Cabrillo and others with him, was heavily edited in later
years by an unknown hand (thus the narrative shifts from the
first to the third person). It tells of the hazards encountered,
most notably the fierce winds and tumultuous ocean threatening sailors in this age when navigation techniques were not
fully developed and ship construction was tenuous.

Herbert Eugene Bolton, ed., *Spanish Exploration of the Southwest, 1542–1706*. New York:
Barnes & Noble, 1963.

Juan Rodriguez set sail from the port of Navidad [on the west coast of Mexico] to explore the coast of New Spain on the 27th of June, 1542.

Between the port of Navidad and Cape Corriente, forty leagues, it took him a day and a night, with a southeast wind. From Wednesday until the following Thursday they held their course along the coast thirty-five leagues.

Sunday, July 2, they sighted [the lower tip of Baja] California. On account of the weather, which was not very favorable, it took them almost four days to cross over. On the following Monday, the 3d of the same month they anchored at the Point of California. . . .

Taking Possession

And thus they sailed along until the next Monday [August 21, 1542], following the coast to the north and northeast; and about ten leagues from Point Engaño [about three-fourths of the way up Baja California] they discovered a good port, in which they cast anchor and took on water and wood. It is in thirty-one and one-half degrees. It is a port suitable for making any kind of repairs on ships, placing them in a secure spot.

On the following Tuesday Captain Juan Rodriguez Cabrillo went ashore, took possession there in the name of his Majesty and of the most Illustrious Señor Don Antonio de Mendoza, and named it port of La Posesion (port of the Possession). He found a lake . . . [and] some Indian fishermen, who forthwith fled. They captured one of them; giving him a few presents they released him and he departed. The interior of the country consists of high and rugged land, but it has good valleys and appears to be good country, although bare. They remained in this place until Sunday, the 27th of said month, repairing the sails and taking on water. On Thursday they saw some smokes and, going to them with the boat, they found some thirty Indian fishermen, who remained where they were. They brought to the ship a boy and two women, gave them clothing and presents, and let them go. From them they could understand nothing by signs.

Signs of Spaniards

On the Friday following, on going to get water, they found in the watering place some Indians who remained quiet and showed them a pool of water, and a saline which contained a large quantity of salt. They said by signs that they did not live there, but inland, and that there were many people. This same day, in the afternoon, five Indians came to the beach; they brought them to the ships and they appeared to be intelligent Indians. Entering the ship they pointed at and counted the Spaniards who were there, and said by signs that they had seen other men like them, who wore beards, and who brought dogs, and crossbows, and swords. The Indians came smeared over with a white paste on the thighs, body, and arms, and wore the paste like slashes, so that they appeared like men in hose and slashed doublets. They made signs that Spaniards were five days from there. They made signs that there were many Indians, and that they had much maize and many parrots. . . .

Afraid of the Europeans

On the following Thursday [September 28] they went about six leagues along a coast running north-northwest, and discovered a port, closed and very good, which they named San Miguel [present-day San Diego]. It is in thirty-four and one-third degrees. Having cast anchor in it, they went ashore where there were people. Three of them waited, but all the rest fled. To these three they gave some presents and they said by signs that in the interior men like the Spaniards had passed. They gave signs of great fear. On the night of this day they went ashore from the ships to fish with a net, and it appears that here there were some Indians, and that they began to shoot at them with arrows and wounded three men.

Next day in the morning they went with the boat farther into the port, which is large, and brought two boys, who understood nothing by signs. They gave them both shirts and sent them away immediately.

Next day in the morning three adult Indians came to the ships and said by signs that in the interior men like us were travelling about, bearded, clothed, and armed like those of the ships. They made signs that they carried crossbows and swords; and they made gestures with the right arm as if they were throwing lances, and ran around as if they were on horseback. They made signs that they were killing many native Indians, and that for this reason they were afraid. These people are comely and large. They go about covered with skins of animals. While they were in this port a heavy storm occurred, but since the port is good they did not feel it at all. It was a violent storm from the west-southwest and the south-southwest. This is the first storm which they have experienced. . . .

Separated by a Storm

At four o'clock this Saturday night [November 11], when lying-to at sea about six leagues from the coast, waiting for morning, with a southeast wind, there blew up so heavy a gale from the southwest and south-southwest, with rain and dark clouds, that they could not carry a palm of sail, and were forced to scud with a small foresail, with much labor, the whole night. On the following Sunday the tempest became much more violent and continued all day, all night, and until noon of the following day. The storm was as severe as any there could be in Spain. On Saturday night they lost sight of their consort.

On Monday, the 13th of said month of November, at the hour of vespers, the wind calmed down and shifted to the west, and at once they set sail and went in search of the consort, steering towards the land, praying to God that they might find her, for they greatly feared that she might be lost. They ran to the north and north-northwest with a wind from the west and west-northwest, and at daybreak on the following Tuesday they sighted the land. They had to run until the afternoon, when they went to reconnoitre a very high coast, and then proceeded along the coast to see if there were any port where they might take shelter. So great was the swell of the ocean that it was terrifying to see, and the coast was bold and the mountains very high. In the afternoon they lay-to for shelter. . . .

On Wednesday, the 15th of said month, they sighted the consort, whereupon they heartily thanked God, for they had thought her lost. They made toward her, and in the afternoon they joined company. Those on the other ship had experienced greater labor and risk than those of the captain's ship, since it was a small vessel and had no deck. This country where they were sailing is apparently very good, but they saw no Indians or smokes. There are large mountains covered with snow, and there is heavy timber. At night they lowered sails and lay-to. . . .

The Search for Shelter

The following Saturday they ran along the coast, and at night found themselves off Cape San Martin [not far from present-day San Francisco]. All the coast run this day is very bold; the sea has a heavy swell, and the coast is very high. There are mountains which reach the sky, and the sea beats upon them. When sailing along near the land, it seems as if the mountains would fall upon the ships. They are covered with snow to the summit, and they named them the Sierras Nevadas. At the beginning of them a cape is formed which projects into the sea, and which they named Cape Nieve [Snow Cape]. The coast runs from north-northwest to south-southeast. It does not appear that Indians live on this coast. This Cape Nieve is in thirty-eight and two-thirds degrees. Whenever the wind blew from the northwest the weather was clear and fair.

On Thursday, the 23d of the month, they arrived, on the return, in the islands of San Lucas, at one of them called La Posesion. They had run the entire coast, point by point, from Cape Pinos to the islands, and had found no shelter whatever, wherefore they were forced to return to said island because during these past days there was a strong wind from the west-northwest, and the swell of the sea was heavy. From Cape Martin to Cape Pinos we did not see a single Indian, the reason being that the coast is bold, rugged, and without shelter. But southeast of Cape Martin for fifteen leagues they found the land inhabited, and with many smokes, because the country is good. . . .

Death of the Captain

Passing the winter on the island of La Posesion, [San Miguel Island, near present-day Santa Barbara] on the 3d of the month of January, 1543, Juan Rodriguez Cabrillo, captain of the said ships, departed from this life, as the result of a fall which he suffered on said island when they were there before, from which he broke an arm near the shoulder [an injury most likely stemming from a battle with natives on the island]. He left as captain the chief pilot, who was one Bartolome Ferrelo, a native of the Levant. At the time of his death he emphatically charged them not to leave off exploring as much as possible of all that coast. They named the island the Island of Juan Rodriguez. . . .

At the Mercy of the Winds

On Friday, the 19th of the said month of January, 1543, they set sail from the island of Juan Rodriguez, which is called Ciquimuymu, to go to the mainland in search of some provisions for their voyage. As they were leaving the port they encountered a heavy wind from the west-northwest, which forced them to seek shelter at the other islands of San Lucas. They anchored at the island of Limun, which they called San Salvador. They were forced to weigh anchor again and depart, because there was no port other than the shelter of the islands. The wind shifted on-shore, and they sailed around these islands eight days with very foul winds, taking shelter from them under the islands themselves; and on the twenty-seventh of said month they entered the same port of the island of Juan Rodriguez where they had been at first. Their greatest difficulty was because the winds were not steady, for they kept changing about from one direction to another. Those most constant are from the west-northwest and west-southwest. . . .

On the following Wednesday, the 28th of said month, at daybreak, the wind shifted directly to the southwest, and did not blow hard. This day they took the latitude in forty-three degrees [near the present-day border between California and Oregon]. Toward night the wind freshened and shifted to the south-southwest. They ran this night to the west-northwest, with great difficulty, and on Thursday, in the morning, the wind shifted to the southwest with great fury, the seas coming from many directions, causing them great fatigue and breaking over the ships; and as they had no decks, if God had not succored them they could not have escaped. Not being able to lay-to, they were forced to scud northeast toward the land; and now, thinking themselves lost, they commended themselves to Our Lady of Guadalupe and made their vows. Thus they ran until three o'clock in the afternoon, with great fear and travail, because they concluded that they were about to be lost, for they saw many signs that land was near by, both birds and very green trees, which came from some rivers, although because the weather was very dark and cloudy the land was invisible. At this hour the Mother of God succored them, by the grace of her Son, for a very heavy rainstorm came up from the north which drove them south with foresails lowered all night and until sunset the next day; and as there was a high sea from the south it broke every time over the prow and swept over them as over a rock. The wind shifted to the northwest and to the north-northwest with great fury, forcing them to scud to the southeast and east-southeast until Saturday the 3d of March, with a sea so high that they became crazed, and if God and his blessed Mother had not miraculously saved them they could not have escaped. On Saturday at midday the wind calmed down and remained in the northwest, for which they gave heartfelt thanks to our Lord. With respect to food they also suffered hardship, because they had nothing but damaged biscuit.

The Return Home

On Monday, the 5th of the month of March, 1543, in the morning, they found themselves at the island of Juan Rodriguez, but they did not dare enter the port because of the high tempest which caused breakers at its entrance in fifteen fathoms. The wind was from the north-northwest. The entrance is narrow. They ran to shelter under the island of San Salvador on the southeast side. The night before, coming with a high tempest, with only two small foresails, they lost sight of the other ship, and feared that she had been swallowed up by the sea; and they were unable to find her again, even in the morning. They think that they must have been in forty-four degrees when struck by the last storm which drove them to shelter. . . .

On Monday, the 2d day of the month of April, they left the island of Cedros to return to New Spain, because they had no supplies with which to again attempt to explore the coast. They arrived in the port of Navidad on Saturday, the 14th day of the said month of April.

Chapter 2

Encountering the Natives

Chapter Preface

O ne of the principal justifications for first seeking out and then governing the inhabitants of the New World was that of religion. Monarchs and church authorities felt the duty to spread Christianity to all peoples of the world. This determination had included, for example, the Spanish war of "reconquest," an endeavor completing a Christian struggle against Muslims dating back to the year 711, when Muslims invaded southern Europe from North Africa. The year Christopher Columbus sailed on his first voyage, in fact, was the year the Spanish Christians defeated the last remaining Muslim forces in Spain.

Similarly, in 1478 Queen Isabella and King Ferdinand instituted the Spanish Inquisition, which continued a line of previous efforts over several centuries to ensure the primacy of Christian beliefs and extinguish "heretical" practices. Methods of enforcement included secret trials, confiscation of property, and public execution. In this way, the Inquisition helped achieve a form of social control over the population. It was in this atmosphere that the exploration and settlement of the New World proceeded, and the emphasis on ensuring and spreading the Christian faith established a connection between conversion of peoples and the conquest of new lands.

The goal of spreading Christianity was not only Spain's. Explorers and settlers from England, France, and Portugal during the fifteenth and sixteenth centuries frequently appealed to their religious duties as justification for their missions. In the early days of exploration of the New World, the Catholic Church and the pope promoted the doctrine that newfound territories would best be governed by Christian rulers who would convert the inhabitants. The papacy played a major role in negotiations between Spain and Portugal in their attempts to establish a boundary dividing any lands discovered in the New World, and each agreed to spread Christianity in these newfound lands.

Yet the methods used by New World representatives of the government to spread Christianity were often sources of contention and were part of the European monarchs' larger struggle to maintain firm control over the possessions. Thousands of miles away, in an age in which communication was slow and reliable information was difficult to obtain, Spanish authorities frequently disapproved of and tried to counteract the actions taken by military and church officials governing the new colonies. Leaders in these new possessions acted increasingly against the expressed authority and approval of the officials back in Europe.

For example, difficulties in asserting the Spanish Crown's authority were rooted in the question of the treatment of the native peoples of the Americas and Caribbean. In Europe there were continuing debates over whether natives were humans with souls and how they should best be "instructed" religiously. Without a clearly defined, officially sanctioned guideline, explorers and settlers began to care less about converting peoples than profiteering from the native workforce. Such men as Bartolomé de Las Casas were not alone in decrying the vicious and destructive methods used by conquerors, officials, and landowners who benefited from native labor. By the 1520s Spanish authorities tried to rein in the abuses of settlers, though their orders and laws were frequently ignored or resisted by settlers in the New World trying to extract as much wealth from the land and the people as possible. But in the case of the islands in the Caribbean, though, there were few people left to convert. By this time the native population originally encountered by Columbus had nearly been wiped out by further contact with the Europeans.

Slaves, Spices, and Gold

Christopher Columbus

Christopher Columbus's expedition in 1492 was only the first of four voyages that the explorer would make. In his second voyage, which lasted from 1493 to 1496, he further explored the Caribbean and tried to establish settlements in what he still thought of as the Indies. A trip in 1496 explored the north coast of South America, and the final expedition in 1502 sent Columbus to the Central American coast, still searching for the elusive strait to Asia.

After the first crossing, Columbus knew that his ability to get approval and financing for additional journeys depended upon his report. Although he found little proof that he had landed in the Indies, lost the flagship Santa Maria on a reef, and faced disloyalty and near mutiny from his crew, the first report he made in the following letter emphasized nothing but success. In it, he refers to the legendary Grand Khan and other signs that the lands he had found were in fact part of Asia. Most importantly, Columbus emphasizes the important future benefits to be had if additional voyages were made. These included rich resources of gold, spices, and, of course, natives, who could be converted to Christianity and easily taken as slaves.

The letter itself was most likely written during Columbus's return passage in 1493. It is addressed to Luís de Santángel, a servant of the crown and important ally of Columbus, but is also intended as an official report to the Spanish monarchs Ferdinand and Isabella.

Christopher Columbus, *Select Documents Illustrating the Four Voyages of Columbus*, edited and translated by Cecil Jane. Nendeln, Liechtenstein: Kraus Reprint Limited, 1967.

S ir, as I know that you will be pleased at the great victory with which Our Lord has crowned my voyage, I write this to you, from which you will learn how in thirty-three days, I passed from the Canary Islands [a convenient stopping point about a week's voyage from Spain] to the Indies with the fleet which the most illustrious king and queen [Ferdinand and Isabella], our sovereigns, gave to me. And there I found very many islands filled with people innumerable, and of them all I have taken possession for their highnesses, by proclamation made and with the royal standard unfurled, and no opposition was offered to me. To the first island which I found, I gave the name *San Salvador*, in remembrance of the Divine Majesty, Who has marvellously bestowed all this; the Indians call it 'Guanahani'. To the second, I gave the name *Isla de Santa María de Concepción*; to the third, *Fernandina*; to the fourth, *Isabella*; to the fifth, *Isla Juana* [now Cuba], and so to each one I gave a new name.

Is This China?

When I reached Juana, I followed its coast to the westward, and I found it to be so extensive that I thought that it must be the mainland, the province of Catayo [in China]. And since there were neither towns nor villages on the seashore, but only small hamlets, with the people of which I could not have speech, because they all fled immediately, I went forward on the same course, thinking that I should not fail to find great cities and towns. And, at the end of many leagues, seeing that there was no change and that the coast was bearing me northwards, which I wished to avoid, since winter was already beginning and I proposed to make from it to the south, and as moreover the wind was carrying me forward, I determined not to wait for a change in the weather and retraced my path as far as a certain harbour known to me. And from that point, I sent two men inland to learn if there were a king or great cities. They travelled three days' journey and found an infinity of small hamlets and people without number, but nothing of importance. For this reason, they returned.

I understood sufficiently from other Indians, whom I had

already taken, that this land was nothing but an island. And therefore I followed its coast eastwards for one hundred and seven leagues to the point where it ended. And from that cape, I saw another island, distant eighteen leagues from the former, to the east, to which I at once gave the name 'Española'. . . .

In this island, there are many spices and great mines of gold and of other metals.

The People of Española

The people of this island, and of all the other islands which I have found and of which I have information, all go naked, men and women, as their mothers bore them, although some women cover a single place with the leaf of a plant or with a net of cotton which they make for the purpose. They have no iron or steel or weapons, nor are they fitted to use them, not because they are not well built men and of handsome stature, but because they are very marvellously timorous. They have no other arms than weapons made of canes, cut in seeding time, to the ends of which they fix a small sharpened stick. And they do not dare to make use of these, for many times it has happened that I have sent ashore two or three men to some town to have speech, and countless people have come out to them, and as soon as they have seen my men approaching they have fled, even a father not waiting for his son. And this, not because ill has been done to anyone; on the contrary, at every point where I have been and have been able to have speech, I have given to them of all that I had, such as cloth and many other things, without receiving anything for it; but so they are, incurably timid. It is true that, after they have been reassured and have lost their fear, they are so guileless and so generous with all they possess, that no one would believe it who has not seen it. They never refuse anything which they possess, if it be asked of them; on the contrary, they invite anyone to share it, and display as much love as if they would give their hearts, and whether the thing be of value or whether it be of small price, at once with whatever trifle of whatever kind it may be that is given to them, with that they are content. I forbade that they should be given things so worthless as fragments of broken crockery and scraps of broken glass, and ends of straps, although when they were able to get them, they fancied that they possessed the best jewel in the world. . . . They took even the pieces of the broken hoops of the wine barrels and, like savages, gave what they had, so that it seemed to me to be wrong and I forbade it. And I gave a thousand handsome good things, which I had brought, in order that they might conceive affection, and more than that, might become Christians and be inclined to the love and service of their highnesses and of the whole Castilian nation, and strive to aid us and to give us of the things which they have in abundance and which are necessary to us. And they do not know any creed and are not idolaters, only they all believe that power and good are in the heavens, and they are very firmly convinced that I, with these ships and men, came from the heavens, and in this belief they everywhere received me, after they had overcome their fear. And this does not come because they are ignorant; on the contrary, they are of a very acute intelligence and are men who navigate all those seas, so that it is amazing how good an account they give of everything, but it is because they have never seen people clothed or ships of such a kind.

Taking Natives by Force

And as soon as I arrived in the Indies, in the first island which I found, I took by force some of them, in order that they might learn and give me information of that which there is in those parts, and so it was that they soon understood us, and we them, either by speech or signs, and they have been very serviceable.[1] I still take them with me, and they are always assured that I come from Heaven, for all the intercourse which they have had with me; and they were the first to announce this wherever I went, and the others went running from house to house and to the neighbouring towns,

1. On his return journey to Spain, Columbus took with him several Indians, of whom only seven survived the voyage. One of these acted as interpreter on the second voyage.

with loud cries of, 'Come! Come to see the people from Heaven!' So all, men and women alike, when their minds were set at rest concerning us, came, so that not one, great or small, remained behind, and all brought something to eat and drink, which they gave with extraordinary affection. . . .

In all these islands, I saw no great diversity in the appearance of the people or in their manners and language. On the contrary, they all understand one another, which is a very curious thing, on account of which I hope that their highnesses will determine upon their conversion to our holy faith, towards which they are very inclined.

I have already said how I have gone one hundred and seven leagues in a straight line from west to east along the seashore of the island Juana, and as a result of that voyage, I can say that this island is larger than England and Scotland together, for, beyond these one hundred and seven leagues, there remain to the westward two provinces to which I have not gone. One of these provinces they call 'Avan', and there the people are born with tails. . . .

Riches and Trade

Española . . . is a land to be desired and, seen, it is never to be left. And in it, although of all I have taken possession for their highnesses and all are more richly endowed than I know how, or am able, to say, and I hold them all for their highnesses, so that they may dispose of them as, and as absolutely as, of the kingdoms of Castile, in this Española, in the situation most convenient and in the best position for the mines of gold and for all intercourse as well with the mainland here as with that there, belonging to the Grand Khan,[2] where will be great trade and gain, I have taken possession of a large town, to which I gave the name *Villa de Navidad*, and in it I have made fortifications and a fort, which now will by this time be entirely finished, and I have left in it sufficient men for such a purpose with arms and artillery and provisions for more than a year, and a *fusta* [small ship], and

2. A powerful ruler who western Europeans still believed dominated the Far East, but who hadn't existed since the fourteenth century.

one, a master of all seacraft, to build others, and great friendship with the king of that land, so much so, that he was proud to call me, and to treat me as, a brother. And even if he were to change his attitude to one of hostility towards these men, he and his do not know what arms are and they go naked, as I have already said, and are the most timorous people that there are in the world, so that the men whom I have left there alone would suffice to destroy all that land, and the island is without danger for their persons, if they know how to govern themselves.

In all these islands, it seems to me that all men are content

Dividends for the Investors

Rather than remember Christopher Columbus and other European explorers solely as one-dimensional heroes who discovered new lands and braved many dangers, many historians also argue the importance of discussing the variety of motives and methods of the Europeans and their effects on the people of these lands. For example, in the following excerpt, historian Howard Zinn tells of Columbus's need to produce a profit—whether in gold or slaves—for those who had sponsored his trips. During his second voyage, from 1493 to 1496, the explorer instituted a violent and deadly system of tribute, forcing the natives into the impossible task of searching for and collecting the supposedly vast amounts of gold that Columbus had described to his patrons.

Now, from his base on Haiti, Columbus sent expedition after expedition into the interior. They found no gold fields, but had to fill up the ships returning to Spain with some kind of dividend. In the year 1495, they went on a great slave raid, rounded up fifteen hundred Arawak [Taino] men, women, and children, put them in pens guarded by Spaniards and dogs, then picked the five hundred best specimens to load onto ships. . . .

But too many of the slaves died in captivity. And so Columbus, desperate to pay back dividends to those who had invested, had to make good his promise to fill the ships with

with one woman, and to their chief or king they give as many as twenty. It appears to me that the women work more than the men. And I have not been able to learn if they hold private property; what seemed to me to appear was that, in that which one had, all took a share, especially of eatable things.

Of Monsters and Cannibals

In these islands I have so far found no human monstrosities, as many expected, but on the contrary the whole population is very well-formed, nor are they negroes as in Guinea, but their hair is flowing, and they are not born where there is in-

---

gold. In the province of Cicao on Haiti, where he and his men imagined huge gold fields to exist, they ordered all persons fourteen years or older to collect a certain quantity of gold every three months. When they brought it, they were given copper tokens to hang around their necks. Indians found without a copper token had their hands cut off and bled to death.

The Indians had been given an impossible task. The only gold around was bits of dust garnered from the streams. So they fled, were hunted down with dogs, and were killed.

Trying to put together an army of resistance, the Arawaks faced Spaniards who had armor, muskets, swords, horses. When the Spaniards took prisoners they hanged them or burned them to death. Among the Arawaks, mass suicides began, with cassava poison. Infants were killed to save them from the Spaniards. In two years, through murder, mutilation, or suicide, half of the 250,000 Indians on Haiti were dead.

When it became clear that there was no gold left, the Indians were taken as slave labor on huge estates, known later as *encomiendas*. They were worked at a ferocious pace, and died by the thousands. By the year 1515, there were perhaps fifty thousand Indians left. By 1550, there were five hundred. A report of the year 1650 shows none of the original Arawaks or their descendants left on the island.

Howard Zinn, *A People's History of the United States, 1492–Present*. Rev. ed. New York: HarperPerennial, 1995.

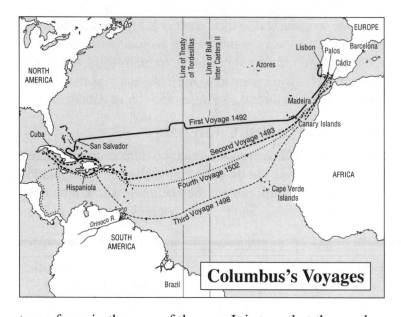

EUROPE

Lisbon Palos Barcelona

Cádiz

Azores

NORTH AMERICA

Line of Treaty of Tordesillas

Line of Bull Inter Caetera II

Madeira

First Voyage 1492

Canary Islands

Cuba

San Salvador

Second Voyage 1493

AFRICA

Hispaniola

Fourth Voyage 1502

Cape Verde Islands

Orinoco R.

Third Voyage 1498

SOUTH AMERICA

Brazil

Columbus's Voyages

tense force in the rays of the sun; It is true that the sun has there great power, although it is distant from the equinoctial line twenty-six degrees. In these islands, where there are high mountains, the cold was severe this winter, but they endure it, being used to it and with the help of meats which they eat with many and extremely hot spices. As I have found no monsters, so I have had no report of any, except in an island 'Quaris', the second at the coming into the Indies, which is inhabited by a people who are regarded in all the islands as very fierce and who eat human flesh. They have many canoes with which they range through all the islands of India and pillage and take as much as they can. They are no more malformed than the others, except that they have the custom of wearing their hair long like women, and they use bows and arrows of the same cane stems, with a small piece of wood at the end, owing to lack of iron which they do not possess. They are ferocious among these other people who are cowardly to an excessive degree, but I make no more account of them than of the rest. These are those who have intercourse with the women of 'Matinino', which is the first island met on the way from Spain to the Indies, in which there is not a man. These women engage in no feminine occupation, but use bows and arrows of cane, like those already mentioned, and they arm and protect themselves with plates of copper, of which they have much.

In another island, which they assure me is larger than Española, the people have no hair. In it, there is gold incalculable, and from it and from the other islands, I bring with me Indians as evidence.

Slaves and Gold

In conclusion, to speak only of that which has been accomplished on this voyage, which was so hasty, their highnesses can see that I will give them as much gold as they may need, if their highnesses will render me very slight assistance; moreover, spice and cotton, as much as their highnesses shall command; and mastic [a useful tree resin], as much as they shall order to be shipped and which, up to now, has been found only in Greece . . . and aloe wood, as much as they shall order to be shipped, and slaves, as many as they shall order to be shipped and who will be from the idolaters. And I believe that I have found rhubarb and cinamon, and I shall find a thousand other things of value, which the people whom I have left there will have discovered. . . .

Since Our Redeemer has given this victory to our most illustrious king and queen, and to their renowned kingdoms, in so great a matter, for this all Christendom ought to feel delight and make great feasts and give solemn thanks to the Holy Trinity with many solemn prayers for the great exaltation which they shall have, in the turning of so many peoples to our holy faith, and afterwards for temporal benefits, for not only Spain but all Christians will have hence refreshment and gain.

"Willing" Christian Converts

Pedro Vaz de Caminha

After explorer Vasco da Gama's historic voyage around the
southern tip of Africa to India (1497–1499), Portugal's King
Manuel I prepared to send another, larger expedition to
expand trade with Asia by the same route. This large fleet
(thirteen ships) was sent in the year 1500 and was commanded by Pedro Álvares Cabral.

Cabral and some of his ships did make the voyage successfully, returning in 1501 after having established trading relationships with kingdoms on the coast of India. Yet for reasons
that are still not entirely clear to historians, before sailing east
around the tip of Africa on the outgoing leg of the journey, the
fleet crossed the Atlantic and landed on the coast of Brazil. This
was possibly the first European presence on that continent.

The fleet stayed there less than two weeks, but a scribe on
the expedition, Pedro Vaz de Caminha, wrote a dispatch to the
king to inform him of the discovery. In the following excerpts
from that letter, he describes the crew's rudimentary commu-
nications with the natives that led the Europeans to believe
that Brazil might contain supplies of gold and other riches.
More tellingly, Caminha also emphasizes to the king the primary source of future "profit" to be found there: a wonderful
supply of new converts to Christianity.

When we were some ten leagues along the coast [of
Brazil] from where we had raised anchor, the small

Pedro Vaz de Caminha, *The Voyages of Pedro Álvares Cabral to Brazil and India*, translated by William Brooks Greenlee. Nendeln, Liechtenstein: Kraus Reprint Limited, 1967.

vessels found a reef within which was a harbour, very good and secure with a very wide entrance. And they went in and lowered their sails. And gradually the ships arrived after them, and a little before sunset they also struck sail about a league from the reef, and anchored in eleven fathoms. And by [Cabral's] order our pilot, Affonso Lopez, who was in one of those small vessels and was an alert and dextrous man for this, straightway entered the skiff to take soundings in the harbour. And he captured two well-built natives who were in a canoe. One of them was carrying a bow and six or seven arrows and many others went about on the shore with bows and arrows and they did not use them. Then, since it was already night, he took the two men to the flagship, where they were received with much pleasure and festivity.

In appearance they are dark, somewhat reddish, with good faces and good noses, well shaped. They go naked, without any covering; neither do they pay more attention to concealing or exposing their shame than they do to showing their faces, and in this respect they are very innocent. Both had their lower lips bored and in them were placed pieces of white bone, the length of a handbreadth, and the thickness of a cotton spindle and as sharp as an awl at the end. They put them through the inner part of the lip, and that part which remains between the lip and the teeth is shaped like a rook in chess. And they carry it there enclosed in such a manner that it does not hurt them, nor does it embarrass them in speaking, eating, or drinking. Their hair is smooth, and they were shorn, with the hair cut higher than above a comb of good size, and shaved to above the ears. And one of them was wearing below the opening, from temple to temple towards the back, a sort of wig of yellow birds' feathers. . . .

Communicating with the Natives

When they came on board, the captain, well dressed, with a very large collar of gold around his neck, was seated in a chair, with a carpet at his feet as a platform. . . . Torches were lighted and they entered, and made no sign of courtesy or of speaking to the captain or to any one, but one of them caught sight of the captain's collar, and began to point with his hand towards the land and then to the collar, as though he were telling us that there was gold in the land. And he also saw a silver candlestick, and in the same manner he made a sign towards the land and then towards the candlestick, as though there were silver also. . . . One of them saw some white rosary beads; he made a motion that they should give them to him, and he played much with them, and put them around his neck; and then he took them off and wrapped them around his arm. He made a sign towards the land and then to the beads and to the collar of the captain, as if to say that they would give gold for that. We interpreted this so, because we wished to, but if he meant that he would take the beads and also the collar, we did not wish to understand because we did not intend to give it to him. . . .

A Sermon

On Low Sunday [the first Sunday after Easter] in the morning the captain determined to go to [a nearby] island to hear mass and a sermon, and he ordered all the captains to assemble in the boats and to go with him; and so it was done. He ordered a large tent to be set up on the island and within it a very well-provided altar to be placed, and there with all the rest of us he had mass said, which the father, Frei Amrique, intoned and all the other fathers and priests who were there accompanied him with the same voice. That mass, in my opinion, was heard by all with much pleasure and devotion. The captain had there with him the banner of Christ, with which he left Belem [a city on the west coast of Portugal], and it was kept raised on the Gospel side. After the mass was finished, the father removed his vestments, and sat down in a high chair, and we all threw ourselves down on that sand, and he preached a solemn and profitable sermon on the history of the Gospel, and at the end of it he dealt with our coming and with the discovery of this land, and referred to the sign of the Cross in obedience to which we came; which was very fitting, and which inspired much devotion.

While we were at mass and at the sermon, about the same

number of people were on the shore as yesterday with their
bows and arrows, who were amusing themselves and watching us; and they sat down, and when the mass was finished
and we were seated for the sermon, many of them arose and
blew a horn or trumpet and began to leap and to dance for a
while. . . .

Then Diogo Dias, who was revenue officer of Sacavem
[and commander of one of the ships], crossed the river. He
is an agreeable and pleasure-loving man, and he took with
him one of our bagpipe players and his bagpipe, and began
to dance among them, taking them by the hands, and they
were delighted and laughed and accompanied him very well
to the sound of the pipe. After they had danced he went
along the level ground, making many light turns and a remarkable leap which astonished them, and they laughed and
enjoyed themselves greatly. And although he reassured and
flattered them a great deal with this, they soon became
sullen like wild men and went away upstream. And then the
captain crossed over the river with all of us, and we went
along the shore, the boats going along close to land, and we
came to a large lake of sweet water which is near the
seashore, because all that shore is marshy above and the water flows out in many places. And after we had crossed the
river some seven or eight of the natives joined our sailors
who were retiring to the boats. . . . Up to this time, although
they were somewhat tamed, a moment afterwards they became frightened like sparrows at a feeding-place. And no
one dared to speak strongly to them for fear they might be
more frightened; and everything was done to their liking in
order to tame them thoroughly. To the old man with whom
the captain spoke he gave a red cap; and in spite of all the
talking that he did with him, and the cap which he gave him,
as soon as he left and began to cross the river, he immediately became more cautious and would not return again to
this side of it. The other two whom the captain had on the
ships, and to whom he gave what has already been mentioned, did not appear again, from which I infer that they are
bestial people and of very little knowledge; and for this rea-

son they are so timid. Yet withal they are well cared for and very clean, and in this it seems to me that they are rather like birds or wild animals, to which the air gives better feathers and better hair than to tame ones. And their bodies are so clean and so fat and so beautiful that they could not be more so; and this causes me to presume that they have no houses or dwellings in which to gather, and the air in which they are

The Requirement

Although thousands of miles from Europe, Spanish settlers and conquerors were subject to the Spanish policies and laws designed to legitimize colonization and conquest. One of these, excerpted below, was the Requerimiento *(the* Requirement, *written in 1512), a proclamation that was to be read aloud (in Spanish) to indigenous people to give them the opportunity to "willingly" accept the religion and authority of their new rulers. In this manner, the conquest could be presented as a missionary activity; for if the natives had been "legally" read these Christian rights and duties and had still refused, the Europeans could then rationalize the use of violence.*

On the part of the King, don Fernando, and of doña Juana, his daughter, Queen of Castille and Leon, subduers of the barbarous nations, we their servants notify and make known to you, as best we can, that the Lord our God, Living and Eternal, created the Heaven and the Earth, and one man and one woman, of whom you and I, and all the men of the world, were and are descendants, and all those who come after us. . . .

Their Highnesses are kings and lords of these islands and land . . . and indeed almost all those to whom this has been notified, have received and served their Highnesses, as lords and kings, in the way that subjects ought to do, with good will, without any resistance, immediately, without delay, when they were informed of the aforesaid facts. . . .

If you do [the same], you will do well, and that which you are obliged to do to their Highnesses, and we in their name brought up makes them so. Nor indeed have we up to this time seen any houses or anything which looks like them. . . .

Trusting the Europeans

On Thursday, the last of April, we ate early in the morning and went on shore for more wood and water, and when the captain was about to leave his ship Sancho de Toar [captain

---

shall receive you in all love and charity, and shall leave you your wives, and your children, and your lands, free without servitude, that you may do with them and with yourselves freely that which you like and think best, and they shall not compel you to turn Christians, unless you yourselves, when informed of the truth, should wish to be converted to our Holy Catholic Faith, as almost all the inhabitants of the rest of the islands have done. And besides this, their Highnesses award you many privileges and exceptions and will grant you many benefits.

But if you do not do this, and wickedly and intentionally delay to do so, I certify to you that, with the help of God, we shall forcibly enter into your country and shall make war against you in all ways and manners that we can, and shall subject you to the yoke and obedience of the Church and of their Highnesses; we shall take you and your wives and your children, and shall make slaves of them, and as such shall sell and dispose of them as their Highnesses may command; and we shall take away your goods, and shall do all the harm and damage that we can, as to vassals who do not obey, and refuse to receive their lord, and resist and contradict him; and we protest that the deaths and losses which shall accrue from this are your fault, and not that of their Highnesses, or ours, nor of these cavaliers who come with us. And that we have said this to you and made this Requirement, we request the notary here present to give us his testimony in writing, and we ask the rest who are present that they should be witnesses of this Requirement.

Lewis Hanke, ed., *History of Latin American Civilization*. vol. 1. Boston: Little, Brown, 1967.

of one of Cabral's ships] arrived with his two [native] guests, and because he had not yet eaten, cloths were laid for him and food was brought, and he ate. We seated the guests in their chairs, and they ate very well of all which was given them, especially of cold boiled ham and rice. They did not give them wine, because Sancho de Toar said that they did not drink it well. After the meal was over we all entered the boat and they with us. . . . When we landed there were probably eight or ten of the natives about, and little by little others began to come. And it seems to me that that day there came to the shore four hundred or four hundred and fifty men. Some of them carried bows and arrows and gave all for caps and for anything which we gave them. They ate with us of what we gave them. Some of them drank wine and others could not drink it, but it seems to me that if they accustomed themselves to it, they would drink it with great willingness. All were so well disposed and so well built and smart with their paints that they made a good show. They loaded as much of that wood as they could, very willingly, and carried it to the boats, and were quieter and more at ease among us than we were among them. . . .

Easy Converts?

When we disembarked, the captain said that it would be well to go directly to the cross, which was leaning against a tree near the river, to be set up the next day, which was Friday, and that we should all kneel down and kiss it so that they might see the respect which we had for it. And thus we did. And we motioned to those ten or twelve who were there that they should do the same, and at once they all went to kiss it. They seem to me people of such innocence that, if one could understand them and they us, they would soon be Christians, because they do not have or understand any belief, as it appears. And therefore, if the convicts[1] who are to remain here will learn their language well and understand

---

1. The fleet carried twenty convicts, or banished men, condemned to death. These were to be landed at desirable places to proselyte the natives and to learn their language. Their success was to be rewarded with pardon.

them, I do not doubt that they will become Christians, in accordance with the pious intent of Your Highness [King Manuel of Portugal], and that they will believe in our Holy Faith, to which may it please Our Lord to bring them. For it is certain this people is good and of pure simplicity, and there can easily be stamped upon them whatever belief we wish to give them; and furthermore, Our Lord gave them fine bodies and good faces as to good men; and He who brought us here, I believe, did not do so without purpose. And consequently, Your Highness, since you so much desire to increase the Holy Catholic Faith, ought to look after their salvation, and it will please God that, with little effort, this will be accomplished.

They do not till the soil or breed stock, nor is there ox or cow, or goat, or sheep, or hen, or any other domestic animal which is accustomed to live with men; nor do they eat anything except these manioc, of which there is much, and of the seeds and the fruits which the earth and the trees produce. Nevertheless, with this they are stronger and better fed than we are with all the wheat and vegetables which we eat.

While they were there that day, they continually skipped and danced with us to the sound of one of our tambours, in such a manner that they are much more our friends than we theirs. If one signed to them whether they wished to come to the ships, they at once made ready to do so, in such wise that had we wished to invite them all, they would all have come. . . .

Planting a Cross

And to-day, which is Friday, the first day of May, we went on land with our banner in the morning and disembarked up the river towards the south, where it seemed to us that it would be better to plant the cross, so that it might be better seen. . . . After the cross was planted with the arms and device of Your Highness which we first nailed to it, we set up an altar at the foot of it. There the father, Frei Amrique, said mass, at which those already mentioned chanted and officiated. There were there with us some fifty or sixty natives, all kneeling as we were, and when it came to the Gospel and we all rose to our feet with hands lifted, they rose with us and lifted their hands, remaining thus until it was over. And then they again sat down as we did. And at the elevation of the Host when we knelt, they placed themselves as we were, with hands uplifted, and so quietly that I assure Your Highness that they gave us much edification. They stayed there with us until communion was over, and after the communion the friars and priests and the captain and some of the rest of us partook of communion. . . . And as it appears to me and to every one, these people in order to be wholly Christian lack nothing except to understand us, for whatever they saw us do, they did likewise; wherefore it appeared to all that they have no idolatry and no worship. And I well believe that, if Your Highness should send here some one who would go about more at leisure among them, that all will be turned to the desire of Your Highness. And if some one should come for this purpose, a priest should not fail to come also at once to baptize them, for by that time they will already have a greater knowledge of our faith through the two convicts who are remaining here among them. Both of these also partook of communion to-day. Among all those who came to-day there was only one young woman who stayed continuously at the mass, and she was given a cloth with which to cover herself, and we put it about her; but as she sat down she did not think to spread it much to cover herself. Thus, Senhor, the innocence of this people is such, that that of Adam could not have been greater in respect to shame. Now Your Highness may see whether people who live in such innocence will be converted or not if they are taught what pertains to their salvation. When this was over we went thus in their presence to kiss the cross, took leave of them, and came to eat. . . .

Future "Profits" in Brazil

It seems to me, Senhor, that this land from the promontory we see farthest south to another promontory which is to the north, of which we caught sight from this harbour, is so great that it will have some twenty or twenty-five leagues of coastline. Along the shore in some places it has great banks, some of them red, some white, and the land above is quite flat and covered with great forests. From point to point the entire shore is very flat and very beautiful. As for the interior, it appeared to us from the sea very large, for, as far as eye could reach, we could see only land and forests, a land which seemed very extensive to us. Up to now we are unable to learn that there is gold or silver in it, or anything of metal or iron; nor have we seen any, but the land itself has a very good climate, . . . because in the present season we found it like that. Its waters are quite endless. So pleasing is it that if one cares to profit by it, everything will grow in it because of its waters. But the best profit which can be derived from it, it seems to me, will be to save this people, and this should be the chief seed which Your Highness should sow there. And if there were nothing more than to have here a stopping-place for this voyage to Calicut [a city in India crucial to the spice trade], that would suffice, to say nothing of an opportunity to fulfil and do that which Your Highness so much desires, namely, the increase of our Holy Faith.

A "Golden Age" in the New World?

Amerigo Vespucci

Historians generally agree that Amerigo Vespucci embarked
on two voyages to the New World: one in 1499 and another in
1501. The second voyage took Vespucci, an Italian and friend
of Columbus, in a fleet of ships from Portugal to the coast of
Brazil. The following account is taken from a letter Vespucci
wrote in 1502 to his patron and former employer in Florence,
Lorenzo di Pier Francesco de' Medici.

An avid geographer and astronomer, Vespucci learned
much about Columbus's claims to have found a passage to the
Indies. In this letter, Vespucci seems to have realized that the
coast he traveled was the edge of a "new" continent and not
an extension of Asia. Additionally, Vespucci was captivated
by the incredible places and people he had encountered. His
descriptions of indigenous people included themes echoed
elsewhere in Renaissance Europe—for example, in the writings of the French essayist Montaigne and in Shakespeare's
play *The Tempest*—in which an idyllic, "Golden Age" way of
living is imagined. In this type of world, the earth voluntarily
yields all that is needed to live, there are no kings to obey,
and private property and greed do not exist. In this way,
Vespucci's description demonstrates as much about the preoc-
cupations and concerns of the people of Europe as it does
about the natives themselves.

Although Columbus had made it to this "new" continent
before Amerigo Vespucci, by 1507 a book and map had been
printed referring to it as "America." Thirty years later, "Amer-

Frederick J. Pohl, ed., *Amerigo Vespucci: Pilot Major*. New York: Octagon Books, 1966.

ica" was applied to the northern continent as well. For
although Columbus might have been the first European in the
New World, Vespucci's efforts verified that "new" meant sep-
arate from Asia, unique, and wondrous.

Your Excellency, My Patron Lorenzo,
                                    after due salutations, etc.
The last letter written to Your Excellency was from the
coast of Guinea from a place which is called Cape Verde. In
it you learned of the beginning of my voyage. By this present letter you will be informed in brief of the middle and end
of my voyage and of what has happened up to now.

We departed from the above-mentioned Cape Verde very
easily, having taken in everything necessary, such as water
and wood and other requirements essential for putting to sea
across the ocean wastes in search of new land. We sailed on
the wind within half a point of southwest, so that in sixty-
four days [delayed by the doldrums (a belt of calm waters
north of the equator)] we arrived at a new land which, for
many reasons that are enumerated in what follows, we observed to be a continent. We ran the course of that land for
about eight hundred leagues, always in the direction of
southwest one-quarter west. ["About eight hundred leagues,"
at four and a half Roman miles a league, was a distance of
about thirty-three hundred English miles.]

We found the land thickly inhabited. I noted there the
wonders of God and of nature, of which I determined to inform Your Excellency, as I have done of my other voyages.

We coursed so far in those seas that we entered the Tor-
rid Zone [an area between the tropics of Cancer and Capri-
corn] and passed south of the equinoctial line and the Tropic
of Capricorn, until the South Pole stood above my horizon
at fifty degrees, which was my latitude from the equator. We
navigated in the Southern Hemisphere for nine months and
twenty-seven days, never seeing the Arctic Pole or even
Ursa Major and Minor; but opposite them many very bright
and beautiful constellations were disclosed to me which al-

ways remain invisible in this Northern Hemisphere. There I noted the wonderful order of their motions and their magnitudes, measuring the diameters of their circuits and mapping out their relative positions with geometrical figures. I noted other great motions of the heavens, which would be a tedious matter to write about. . . .

Descriptions of Wonder

Let us describe the country and the inhabitants and the animals and the plants and the other things I found in their habitations which are of general usefulness to human living.

This land is very pleasing, full of an infinite number of very tall trees which never lose their leaves and throughout the year are fragrant with the sweetest aromas and yield an endless supply of fruits, many of which are good to taste and conducive to bodily health. The fields produce many herbs and flowers and most delicious and wholesome roots. Sometimes I was so wonder-struck by the fragrant smells of the herbs and flowers and the savor of the fruits and the roots that I fancied myself near the Terrestrial Paradise. What shall we say of the multitude of birds and their plumes and colors and singing and their numbers and their beauty? I am unwilling to enlarge upon this description, because I doubt if I would be believed.

What should I tell of the multitude of wild animals, the abundance of pumas, of panthers, of wild cats, not like those of Spain, but of the antipodes; of so many wolves, red deer, monkeys, and felines, marmosets of many kinds, and many large snakes? We saw so many other animals that I believe so many species could not have entered Noah's ark. [A heretical and quite dangerous doubt; long experience with the limited space on shipboard helped to make him skeptical.] We saw many wild hogs, wild goats, stags and does, hares, and rabbits, but of domestic animals, not one.

Is This the Golden Age?

Let us come to rational animals. We found the whole land inhabited by people entirely naked, the men like the women without any covering of their shame. Their bodies are very agile and well proportioned, of light color, with long hair, and little or no beard. I strove a great deal to understand their conduct and customs. For twenty-seven days I ate and slept among them, and what I learned about them is as follows.

Having no laws and no religious faith, they live according to nature. They understand nothing of the immortality of the soul. There is no possession of private property among them, for everything is in common. They have no boundaries of kingdom or province. They have no king, nor do they obey anyone. Each one is his own master. There is no administration of justice, which is unnecessary to them, because in their code no one rules. They live in communal dwellings, built in the fashion of very large cabins. For people who have no iron or indeed any metal, one can call their cabins truly miraculous houses. For I have seen habitations which are two hundred and twenty paces long and thirty wide, ingeniously fabricated; and in one of these houses dwelt five or six hundred persons. They sleep in nets woven out of cotton, going to bed in mid-air with no other coverture. They eat squatting upon the ground. Their food is very good: an endless quantity of fish; a great abundance of sour cherries, shrimps, oysters, lobsters, crabs, and many other products of the sea. The meat which they eat most usually is what one may call human flesh a la mode. When they can get it, they eat other meat, of animals or birds, but they do not lay hold of many, for they have no dogs, and the country is a very thick jungle full of ferocious wild beasts. For this reason they are not wont to penetrate the jungle except in large parties.

Native Customs

The men have a custom of piercing their lips and cheeks and setting in these perforations ornaments of bone or stone; and do not suppose them small ones. Most of them have at least three holes, and some seven, and some nine, in which they set ornaments of green and white alabaster, half a palm in length and as thick as a Catalonian plum. This pagan custom is beyond description. They say they do this to make themselves look more fierce. In short, it is a brutal business.

Their marriages are not with one woman only, but they mate with whom they desire and without much ceremony. I know a man who had ten women. He was jealous of them, and if it happened that one of them was guilty, he punished her and sent her away. They are a very procreative people. They do not have heirs, because they do not have private property. When their children, that is, the females, are of age to procreate, the first who seduces one has to act as her father in place of the nearest relative. After they are thus violated, they marry.

Their women do not make any ceremony over childbirth, as do ours, but they eat all kinds of food, and wash themselves up to the very time of delivery, and scarcely feel any pain in parturition. [This statement that Indian women wash themselves during pregnancy was most startling to Europeans, who believed in the superstitious custom of unclean motherhood.]

They are a people of great longevity, for according to their way of attributing issue, they had known many men who had four generations of descendants. They do not know how to compute time in days, months, and years, but reckon time by lunar months. When they wished to demonstrate something involving time, they did it by placing pebbles, one for each lunar month. I found a man of advanced age who indicated to me with pebbles that he had seen seventeen hundred lunar months, which I judged to be a hundred and thirty-two years, counting thirteen moons to the year.

A Warlike People

They are also a warlike people and very cruel to their own kind. All their weapons and the blows they strike are, as [14th-century Italian poet] Petrarch says, "committed to the wind," for they use bows and arrows, darts, and stones. They use no shields for the body, but go into battle naked. They have no discipline in the conduct of their wars, except that they do what their old men advise. When they fight, they slaughter mercilessly. . . . That which made me the more astonished at their wars and cruelty was that I could not understand from them why they made war upon each other, considering that they held no private property or sovereignty of empire and kingdoms and did not know any such thing as lust for possession, that is, pillaging or a desire to rule, which appear to me to be the causes of wars and of every disorderly act. When we requested them to state the cause, they did not know how to give any other cause than that this curse upon them began in ancient times and they sought to avenge the deaths of their forefathers. In short, it is a brutal business. . . .

As to the nature of the land, I declare it to be the most agreeable, temperate, and healthful, for in all the time that we were in it, which was ten months, none of us died and only a few fell ill. As I have already said, the inhabitants live a long time and do not suffer from infirmity or pestilence or from any unhealthy atmosphere. Death is from natural causes or from the hand of man. In conclusion, physicians would have a wretched standing in such a place.

The Benefits of Discovery

Because we went solely to make discoveries, and departed from Lisbon [Portugal] with a commission to that effect, and not to seek for any profit, we did not trouble ourselves to search the land or look for any gain. Thus we did not perceive in it anything that would be profitable to anyone; not because I do not believe that the land might not produce every kind of wealth, from its wonderful nature and from the climate of the region in which it is situated. It is not surprising that we did not at once become sensible of everything there that might make for profit, since the inhabitants value neither gold nor silver nor precious stones—nothing but feathers and the previously mentioned ornaments made of bone. I hope that this Serene King will send an expedition now to inspect it and that before many years pass it will bring to this kingdom of Portugal a handsome profit and a yearly income.

We found an endless growth of very good dyewood, enough to load all the ships that nowadays sail the seas, and free from cost. The same is true of the cassia fistula [a medicinal plant].

We saw crystals and a great variety of savory and fragrant spices and drugs, but their properties are not known. The natives told us of gold and other metals and many miracle-working drugs, but I am one of those followers of Saint Thomas, who are slow to believe. Time will reveal everything.

The sky was clear there most of the time, and aglow with many bright stars, and I made notes on all of these, with their circuits. This is only a brief outline and a mere list of the things I saw in that country. Many things have been omitted, in order not to be wearisome and because you will find them in complete detail in my account of the voyage.

In Defense of the Natives

Bartolomé de Las Casas

Fundamental questions facing Europeans in the New World concerned the nature of its inhabitants. Were they humans, capable of rational thought? Could they fully receive the benefits of Christianity? How should they be treated?

Like many, historian, theologian, and "Defender of the Indians" Bartolomé de Las Casas initially believed that the natives should be exploited as the invaders saw fit. He first arrived on Hispaniola (the Caribbean island site of present-day Haiti and the Dominican Republic) in 1502 as a young man to oversee land granted to his father, who had accompanied Columbus on his second voyage. Later Las Casas managed his own *encomienda*: a grant of land upon which a settler could put natives to work—essentially as slaves—in exchange for taking charge of their religious instruction. This system led to terrible exploitation, as settlers sought to extract the maximum profit while showing little regard for their native workers.

Las Casas, however, experienced a major change of heart in 1514. In *A Short Account of the Destruction of the Indies*, published in 1542 but based on principles he began advocating much earlier, Las Casas pleads for the reformation of Spanish policy and practice toward New World natives. In the 1542 text, from which the following passages are taken, Las Casas relies upon several arguments: he states that the natives are rational human beings with unique civilizations of their own; he offers empirical, firsthand accounts of destruction

Bartolomé de Las Casas, *A Short Account of the Destruction of the Indies*, edited and translated by Nigel Griffin. New York: Penguin Books, 1992. Copyright © 1992 by Anthony Pagden. Reproduced by permission of the publisher.

wrought by Europeans and estimates of the numbers of people killed; and he contrasts the friendly behavior of the natives with that of the greedy and violent invaders. In doing so, he provided a forceful voice insisting on the rights of natives—a radical message for Renaissance Europe.

M ost high and most mighty Lord [Prince Philip of Spain]:

As Divine Providence has ordained that the world shall, for the benefit and proper government of the human race, be divided into kingdoms and peoples and that these shall be ruled by kings, who are . . . fathers and shepherds to their people and are, accordingly, the noblest and most virtuous of beings, there is no doubt, nor could there in all reason be any such doubt, but that these kings entertain nothing save that which is morally unimpeachable. It follows that if the commonwealth suffers from some defect, or shortcoming, or evil, the reason can only be that the ruler is unaware of it; once the matter is brought to his notice, he will work with the utmost diligence to set matters right and will not rest content until the evil has been eradicated. . . .

An Appeal to the Prince

Contemplating, therefore (most mighty Lord), as a man with more than fifty years' experience of seeing at first hand the evil and the harm, the losses and diminutions suffered by those great kingdoms, each so vast and so wonderful that it would be more appropriate to refer to them as the New World of the Americas—kingdoms granted and entrusted by God and His Church to the Spanish Crown so that they might be properly ruled and governed, converted to the Faith, and tenderly nurtured to full material and spiritual prosperity—I am persuaded that, if Your Highness had been informed of even a few of the excesses which this New World has witnessed, all of them surpassing anything that men hitherto have imagined even in their wildest dreams, Your Highness would not have delayed for even one moment before entreating His Majesty to prevent any repetition of the atrocities which go under the name of 'conquests': excesses which, if no move is made to stop them, will be committed time and again, and which (given that the indigenous peoples of the region are naturally so gentle, so peace-loving, so humble and so docile) are of themselves iniquitous, tyrannical, contrary to natural, canon, and civil law, and are deemed wicked and are condemned and proscribed by all such legal codes. I therefore concluded that it would constitute a criminal neglect of my duty to remain silent about the enormous loss of life as well as the infinite number of human souls despatched to Hell in the course of such 'conquests', and so resolved to publish an account of a few such outrages (and they can be only a few out of the countless number of such incidents that I could relate) in order to make that account the more accessible to Your Highness. . . .

This, Your Royal Highness, is a matter on which action is both urgent and necessary if God is to continue to watch over the Crown of Castile and ensure its future well-being and prosperity, both spiritual and temporal. Amen.

The Natural Goodness of the Natives

The Americas were discovered in 1492, and the first Christian settlements established by the Spanish the following year. It is accordingly forty-nine years now since Spaniards began arriving in numbers in this part of the world. They first settled the large and fertile island of Hispaniola, which boasts six hundred leagues [about 1560 miles] of coastline and is surrounded by a great many other large islands, all of them, as I saw for myself, with as high a native population as anywhere on earth. Of the coast of the mainland, which, at its nearest point, is a little over two hundred and fifty leagues from Hispaniola, more than ten thousand leagues had been explored by 1541, and more are being discovered every day. This coastline, too, was swarming with people and it would seem, if we are to judge by those areas so far explored, that the Almighty selected this part of the world as home to the greater part of the human race.

God made all the peoples of this area, many and varied as they are, as open and as innocent as can be imagined. The simplest people in the world—unassuming, long-suffering, unassertive, and submissive—they are without malice or guile, and are utterly faithful and obedient both to their own native lords and to the Spaniards in whose service they now find themselves. Never quarrelsome or belligerent or boisterous, they harbour no grudges and do not seek to settle old scores; indeed, the notions of revenge, rancour, and hatred are quite foreign to them. At the same time, they are among the least robust of human beings: their delicate constitutions make them unable to withstand hard work or suffering and render them liable to succumb to almost any illness, no matter how mild. Even the common people are no tougher than princes or than other Europeans born with a silver spoon in their mouths and who spend their lives shielded from the rigours of the outside world. They are also among the poorest people on the face of the earth; they own next to nothing and have no urge to acquire material possessions. As a result they are neither ambitious nor greedy, and are totally uninterested in worldly power. Their diet is every bit as poor and as monotonous, in quantity and in kind, as that enjoyed by the Desert Fathers. Most of them go naked, save for a loincloth to cover their modesty; at best they may wrap themselves in a piece of cotton material a yard or two square. Most sleep on matting, although a few possess a kind of hanging net, known in the language of Hispaniola as a hammock. They are innocent and pure in mind and have a lively intelligence, all of which makes them particularly receptive to learning and understanding the truths of our Catholic faith and to being instructed in virtue; indeed, God has invested them with fewer impediments in this regard than any other people on earth. . . .

Genocide in the New World

It was upon these gentle lambs, imbued by the Creator with all the qualities we have mentioned, that from the very first day they clapped eyes on them the Spanish fell like ravening wolves upon the fold, or like tigers and savage lions who have not eaten meat for days. The pattern established at the outset has remained unchanged to this day, and the Spaniards still do nothing save tear the natives to shreds, murder them and inflict upon them untold misery, suffering and distress, tormenting, harrying and persecuting them mercilessly. We shall in due course describe some of the many ingenious methods of torture they have invented and refined for this purpose, but one can get some idea of the effectiveness of their methods from the figures alone. When the Spanish first journeyed there, the indigenous population of the island of Hispaniola stood at some three million; today only two hundred survive. The island of Cuba, which extends for a distance almost as great as that separating Valladolid from Rome, is now to all intents and purposes uninhabited; and two other large, beautiful and fertile islands, Puerto Rico and Jamaica, have been similarly devastated. Not a living soul remains today on any of the islands of the Bahamas, which lie to the north of Hispaniola and Cuba, even though every single one of the sixty or so islands in the group, as well as those known as the Isles of Giants and others in the area, both large and small, is more fertile and more beautiful than the Royal Gardens in Seville and the climate is as healthy as anywhere on earth. The native population, which once numbered some five hundred thousand, was wiped out by forcible expatriation to the island of Hispaniola, a policy adopted by the Spaniards in an endeavour to make up losses among the indigenous population of that island. . . .

At a conservative estimate, the despotic and diabolical behaviour of the Christians has, over the last forty years, led to the unjust and totally unwarranted deaths of more than twelve million souls, women and children among them, and there are grounds for believing my own estimate of more than fifteen million to be nearer the mark.

Greed and Murder

There are two main ways in which those who have travelled to this part of the world pretending to be Christians have uprooted these pitiful peoples and wiped them from the face of the earth. First, they have waged war on them: unjust, cruel, bloody and tyrannical war. Second, they have murdered anyone and everyone who has shown the slightest sign of resistance, or even of wishing to escape the torment to which they have subjectd him. . . .

The reason the Christians have murdered on such a vast scale and killed anyone and everyone in their way is purely and simply greed. They have set out to line their pockets with gold and to amass private fortunes as quickly as possible so that they can then assume a status quite at odds with that into which they were born. Their insatiable greed and overweening ambition know no bounds; the land is fertile and rich, the inhabitants simple, forbearing and submissive. The Spaniards have shown not the slightest consideration for these people, treating them (and I speak from first-hand experience, having been there from the outset) not as brute animals—indeed, I would to God they had done and had shown them the consideration they afford their animals—so much as piles of dung in the middle of the road. They have had as little concern for their souls as for their bodies, all the millions that have perished having gone to their deaths with no knowledge of God and without the benefit of the Sacraments. One fact in all this is widely known and beyond dispute, for even the tyrannical murderers themselves acknowledge the truth of it: the indigenous peoples never did the Europeans any harm whatever; on the contrary, they believed them to have descended from the heavens, at least until they or their fellow-citizens had tasted, at the hands of these oppressors, a diet of robbery, murder, violence, and all other manner of trials and tribulations. . . .

Futile Resistance on Hispaniola

It all began with the Europeans taking native women and children both as servants and to satisfy their own base appetites; then, not content with what the local people offered them of their own free will (and all offered as much as they could spare), they started taking for themselves the food the natives contrived to produce by the sweat of their brows, which was in all honesty little enough. Since what a European will consume in a single day normally supports three native households of ten persons each for a whole month, and since the newcomers began to subject the locals to other vexations, assaults, and iniquities, the people began to realize that these men could not, in truth, have descended from the heavens. . . . It was then that the locals began to think up ways of driving the Europeans out of their lands and to take up arms against them. Their weapons, however, were flimsy and ineffective both in attack and in defence (and, indeed, war in the Americas is no more deadly than our jousting, or than many European children's games) and, with their horses and swords and lances, the Spaniards easily fended them off, killing them and committing all kind of atrocities against them.

They forced their way into native settlements, slaughtering everyone they found there, including small children, old men, pregnant women, and even women who had just given birth. They hacked them to pieces, slicing open their bellies with their swords as though they were so many sheep herded into a pen. They even laid wagers on whether they could manage to slice a man in two at a stroke, or cut an individual's head from his body, or disembowel him with a single blow of their axes. They grabbed suckling infants by the feet and, ripping them from their mothers' breasts, dashed them headlong against the rocks. Others, laughing and joking all the while, threw them over their shoulders into a river, shouting: 'Wriggle, you little perisher.' They slaughtered anyone and everyone in their path, on occasion running through a mother and her baby with a single thrust of their swords. They spared no one, erecting especially wide gibbets on which they could string their victims up with their feet just off the ground and then burn them alive thirteen at a time, in honour of our Saviour and the twelve Apostles, or tie dry straw to their bodies and set fire to it. . . .

Unique Civilizations

On Hispaniola there were five main kingdoms, each very extensive and each with its own king; most of the infinite number of local nobles paid allegiance to one or other of these five powerful leaders, although there were a few backwoodsmen who recognized no authority above and beyond their own. One of these kingdoms was called Maguá, with the stress on the last syllable which means Kingdom of the Plain. This plain is one of the wonders of the world, extending, as it does, for some eighty leagues, right from the southern coast of the island to its northern shore. For the most part it is some five to eight leagues wide and as much as ten in places, and is confined by high mountains on either side. Over thirty thousand streams and rivers flow into it, a dozen of them every bit as big as the Ebro, Duero, and Guadalquivir [the three principal rivers of Spain], and those that come down from the mountains to the west (and there are twenty or twenty-five thousand of them) are rich in alluvial gold. Among those mountains lies the province of Cibao and its mines, famous throughout the region for their very high-quality gold. The king of Cibao was called Guarionex and he had as vassals several extremely powerful local leaders; one of them, for example, had sixteen thousand men under arms and these he placed at the service of Guarionex. I met some of these men myself. The king himself was dutiful and virtuous, a man of placid temperament much devoted to the King and Queen of Spain. For a number of years, every householder throughout his realm made, on his orders, an annual gift of a hollow gourd completely filled with gold. The natives of Hispaniola know little of mining techniques and later, when there was less gold available, the king reduced this offering to half a gourd filled with gold. In order to put a stop to the Spaniards' incessant demands for gold, Guarionex suggested that he might better serve the King of Castile by putting a great area of his kingdom under cultivation, especially as his subjects had, as he himself quite correctly asserted, little or no notion of how to mine for gold. Such a plan was feasible, as I can vouch, and the king would have been quite happy to see it put into effect. . . .

The wicked European commanders rewarded this good

and great man by dishonouring him when one of their number [Francisco Roldán, one of the companions of Columbus]
took and raped his wife. To this the king could easily have
reacted by biding his time and gathering an army to exact revenge, but he elected instead to abdicate and go into volun-
tary exile, alone, to an area called Ciguayos, where the powerful local leader was one of his vassals. Once the Europeans
realized he had gone, there was no chance of keeping his
whereabouts secret, and they got up an army and attacked the
local leader under whose protection the king was sheltering.
The carnage was terrible and, eventually, they tracked down
the fugitive, took him prisoner, put him in chains and shack-
les and bundled him on to a ship bound for Castile, only for
him to perish, along with many Spaniards, when the ship was
lost at sea [in 1502]. A fortune in gold sank beneath the
waves that day, among the cargo being the Great Nugget, as
big as a loaf of bread and weighing three thousand six hundred *castilians*. In this way, God passed judgement on the
great iniquities committed by the Spanish.

They Had Welcomed Columbus

Another of these original kingdoms occupied the northern
end of the plain where the royal harbour is today. Known as
Marién, it was a rich region, larger than Portugal, although
a good deal more fertile and far better suited to human habi-
tation, criss-crossed as it is by several mighty mountain
ranges and seamed with productive gold and copper mines.
The king of this area was called Guacanagarí with the stress
on the last syllable, and he numbered among his vassals
many men of high standing, several of whom I knew personally. This was the first place where the old Admiral
[Columbus] who discovered the New World first landed and
was received on that occasion by this Guacanagarí, as were
all his crew, with the greatest kindness and humanity imag-
inable. As Columbus himself told me, it was there that the
Admiral's own ship was lost [in 1492] and he and his men
were as graciously treated and looked after as if they had
been back home and were all part of the same close family.

Guacanagarí himself died up in the mountains, broken and destitute, after he had fled to escape the massacres and the cruelty inflicted by the Spaniards, and all the other local leaders who owed allegiance to Guacanagarí perished as a direct result of the despotism and slavery to which they were subjected and which I shall in due course set out in detail.

The third of these kingdoms was the sovereign state of Maguana, another strikingly beautiful and fertile area and one which enjoyed the healthiest of climates. It is this area that nowadays produces the best sugar on the whole island. The king, Caonabó, who outdid all others in strength, majesty of bearing and court ceremonial, was captured by an underhand trick and taken from his own house. He was put on board one of the Spanish ships bound for Castile; but the Almighty determined not to allow this act of duplicity and injustice to pass unnoticed and, that night, sent a violent storm in which all six of the ships, still in harbour and on the very point of setting sail, sank with the loss of all hands. Caonabó, shackled and chained as he was, perished along with them. . . .

Injustices Against a Noble People

The fourth kingdom was known as Xaraguá, and was really the heart and core of the whole island. In no other part of the island was the language as refined as here nor the court discourse as cultivated; nowhere else were the people of such quality and breeding, the leading families as numerous and as liberal—and this kingdom boasted many nobles and great lords—nor the inhabitants as handsome and easy on the eye. Chief among them were the king, Behechio, and his sister, Anacaona, both of whom rendered great service to the Spanish Crown and gave every assistance to the European settlers, on occasion even saving their lives; after Behechio's death, Anacaona ruled in his stead. Over three hundred local dignitaries were summoned to welcome the then governor of the island when he paid a visit to the kingdom with sixty horse and a further three hundred men on foot (the horsemen alone were sufficient in number to ravage not only the whole island but the mainland as well). The governor duped the unsuspecting leaders of this welcoming party into gathering in a building made of straw and then ordered his men to set fire to it and burn them alive. All the others were massacred, either run through by lances or put to the sword. As a mark of respect and out of deference to her rank, Queen Anacaona was hanged. . . .

The fifth kingdom was known as Higuey and its queen, a lady already advanced in years, went by the name of Higuanama. They strung her up and I saw with my own eyes how the Spaniards burned countless local inhabitants alive or hacked them to pieces, or devised novel ways of torturing them to death, enslaving those they took alive. Indeed, they invented so many new methods of murder that it would be quite impossible to set them all down on paper and, however hard one tried to chronicle them, one could probably never list a thousandth part of what actually took place. . . .

The Survivors Become Slaves

After the fighting was over and all the men had been killed, the surviving natives—usually, that is, the young boys, the women, and the children—were shared out between the victors. One got thirty, another forty, a third as many as a hundred or even twice that number; everything depended on how far one was in the good books of the despot who went by the title of governor. The pretext under which the victims were parcelled out in this way was that their new masters would then be in a position to teach them the truths of the Christian faith; and thus it came about that a host of cruel, grasping and wicked men, almost all of them pig-ignorant, were put in charge of these poor souls. And they discharged this duty by sending the men down the mines, where working conditions were appalling, to dig for gold, and putting the women to labour in the fields and on their master's estates, to till the soil and raise the crops, properly a task only for the toughest and strongest of men. Both women and men were given only wild grasses to eat and other unnutritious foodstuffs. The mothers of young children promptly saw their milk dry up and their babies die; and, with the women and the men separated and never seeing each other, no new children were born. The men died down the mines from overwork and starvation, and the same was true of the women who perished out on the estates. The islanders, previously so numerous, began to die out as would any nation subjected to such appalling treatment.

Chapter 3

Conquest

Chapter Preface

In his firsthand account of Spaniard Hernán Cortés's 1519 to 1521 conquest of Mexico, soldier and chronicler Bernal Díaz wrote of the sheer numbers of warriors faced by the Spanish invaders. Yet in one particularly fierce battle of four hundred Spaniards facing thousands of Aztecs, Díaz reported that only one conqueror was killed. Díaz surmised that the enemy was not "well commanded," but he also gave another reason for the victory: "The steady bearing of our artillery, musketeers and crossbowmen, was indeed a help to us, and we did the enemy much damage." Such battles pitting relatively small numbers of Europeans against larger armies of native peoples were replayed often in the initial years of conquest and settlement of the New World—from the army of Francisco Pizarro in Peru to the soldiers commanded by Hernando de Soto in La Florida. As Díaz's account suggests, though, one reason for the victories of the outnumbered invaders had to do with their superior weaponry.

The methods and armaments used in battle by the native peoples varied from region to region and at various points in the conquest of the New World, as did the techniques and resources available to the invaders. Nevertheless, the Europeans generally fought using gunpowder, crossbows, and armor, and the defenders relied upon arrows, spears, and, at times, swords. One main advantage for the attackers was the use of shoulder arms such as the arquebus, a small-caliber rifle that fired shot, a spray of lead balls that could kill or wound more than one enemy. From a larger distance, the Europeans could also attack or frighten native soldiers with their cannons mounted on ships. The superior armor of the conquerors also meant that even when native soldiers did approach close enough to make an attack, their weapons were frequently ineffective.

In addition, the Europeans had several other advantages.

For example, in Cortés's march toward the capital of Mexico, part of his army was mounted on horses. Not only did the advantage of speed, maneuverability, and height aid the horsemen, but because horses were not native to the New World, the indigenous people were often awed and frightened by these strange beasts. Settlers and conquerors also used vicious dogs in the control of native populations. Additionally, they brought new diseases—such as smallpox, measles, and cholera—that the native peoples had never encountered, and many succumbed easily to this microscopic weapon.

Although greatly outnumbered—the native population of the West Indies at the time of Columbus's arrival, for example, is estimated to have been several million—the invaders had one additional advantage. Especially in the early years, the inclination of native peoples was to welcome and assist the explorers and settlers. And even after they had experienced many examples of the Europeans' cruelty, discrete villages, tribes, and peoples were rarely able to unite in opposition. In fact, Cortés's army relied heavily on thousands of native warriors willing to band with Cortés to free themselves from Aztec rule. Without these allies, Cortés could never have succeeded. And, as in the case of Cortés's march on the Aztec Empire and its leader, Montezuma, the natives were never entirely sure of what to make of the newcomers. Were they friends or foe? Could they actually pose a serious threat with their small army? Was it possible that Cortés was really Quetzalcoatl, a semilegendary ruler prophesied to return? This confusion prevented Montezuma from mounting any concentrated and sustained defense and, coupled with the technological superiority and efficacy of the strange invaders and their germs, helped pave the way for the conquest of the New World.

Power Struggles in the New World

Vasco Núñez de Balboa

Vasco Núñez de Balboa arrived in the New World by 1500 and participated in conquering expeditions and the founding of Spanish settlements in the peninsular regions connecting South America and Central America, specifically Panama and Darién. He is widely remembered for being among the first (if not *the* first) Europeans to find the Pacific Ocean and claim it on behalf of his monarchs.

Under Balboa's leadership, the settlement at Darién was more secure and prosperous than others, and even absorbed the haggard survivors of two failed outposts, which, according to Balboa, had been mismanaged by their leaders, Diego de Nicuesa (Niquesa in the following text) and Alonso de Ojeda. For officials such as Balboa, conquering natives and securing adequate provisions also required outmaneuvering fellow Spaniards in the colonies, as each attempted to increase his own local power while gaining royal backing. Balboa wrote the following appeal to King Ferdinand in 1513 in hopes of both solidifying his own authority and ensuring the survival of his settlement. In this letter, Balboa denigrates his opponents, lauds his own abilities, and boldly presumes to instruct the king as to what actions should be taken in the New World. Although the king responded favorably by sending a relief expedition, Balboa soon lost the New World power struggle and was executed by a rival in 1519.

Charles L.G. Anderson, *Life and Letters of Vasco Núñez de Balboa*. New York: Fleming H. Revell Company, 1941.

And the nature of the land is such that if he who has charge of governing it sleeps, when he wishes to wake he cannot, because it is a country which requires that he who rules it pass over and around it many times; and as the land is very difficult to travel over on account of the many rivers and extensive marshes and mountains where many men die from the great toil suffered, it causes one to experience bad nights and endure fatigues, for every day it is necessary to face death a thousand times; and for this reason they like to excuse themselves with some persons who do not care much whether they do well or ill, like Diego de Niquesa[1] has done, for which reason he was lost, as well the one as the other; and in order that Your Most Royal Highness may know by whom Diego de Niquesa was ruled and by what person he was exonerated, I am sending you an information of all that occurred, by which Your Most Royal Highness will see the affairs as they were conducted and how I was able to do that which was conducive to the said service of God and of Your Most Royal Highness: the greater part of their perdition has been due to the bad treatment of their people [European settlers], for they believe that once they had them here that they were held as slaves, because even with the things that were taken to eat on the forays they were unfairly treated, as much in the government of Alonso de Ojeda[2] as in that of Diego de Niquesa, and never of whatever gold that was taken nor of the other things were they given the value of a *real;* for which reason everybody went about so despondent that although they saw the gold alongside they did not care to take it, knowing that they would have little share of it.

Balboa's Leadership

I wish to make known to Your Royal Majesty the reason why I have obtained and know the great secrets which are in this land. . . . Above all, I have striven whithersoever I

---

1. Niquesa [or Nicuesa] was the failed governor of settlements in the Western portion of Tierra Firme, or northern South America.   2. Ojeda had been governor of the eastern section of Tierra Firme, known as Urabá.

have gone that the Indians of this land be very well treated, not consenting to do them any harm, dealing with them truthfully, and giving them many articles from Spain to attract them to our friendship. Treating them honestly has been the cause that I have learned very great secrets from them and things whereby one can secure very great riches and large quantity of gold, with which Your Most Royal Highness will be very much served. . . .

I, my Lord, have sought constantly to make very honest division of all that has been taken to the present time of gold, *guanin* [another precious metal], and pearls, first putting aside what belongs to Your Most Royal Highness, as well as all the other things, like Indian cloth and things to eat: for until now we have cherished things to eat more than the gold, because we have more gold than health; for many times I was in places where I was more pleased to find a basket of corn than another of gold, accordingly, I assure Your Most Royal Highness that continually we have needed food more than the gold.

I certify to Your Most Royal Highness that if I in person had not marched at the head of my men looking for food for those who went with me and for those who remained in this Town, it would be a wonder if anyone remained in the Town or in this land, in case our Lord might not miraculously show mercy with us. . . .

Balboa's Discoveries

Most puissant Lord, that which I with great industry and much labor by good fortune have discovered is this:—

In this province of Darien are found many very rich mines, there is gold in much quantity: twenty rivers have been explored, and thirty which contain gold issue from a ridge of mountains which is about two leagues from this Town, running toward the region of the south. . . .

Going up this great river [Atrato] thirty leagues, on the left hand enters a very large and beautiful river, and two days journey up this river is a Cacique who is called *Davaive* [or Davaibe]: he is a very great Lord of a very large territory thickly settled with people. He has gold in great quantity in his house, and so much that for one who does not know the things of this land it will be quite dubious to believe. . . .

Two days' march from there is a very beautiful country in which is a very evil Carib people, they eat as many men as they can get: this people is without a Lord and they have no one to obey, they are warlike and each one lives for himself alone. These people are Lords of the mines, and these mines according to the news I have, are the richest in the world. . . .

They say that the Indians of the other coast [i.e. the Pacific coast] are very sociable and polite: they tell me that the other sea is very good to navigate in canoes, for it is continually smooth and never rough like the sea on their side, according to what the Indians say: I believe that in that sea are many islands where are many rich pearls in abundance, and that the Caciques [chiefs] have baskets full of them, as well as have all the Indians, men and women, generally. . . .

Since our Lord has made you the Master of such a great land where so much treasure is, it must not be cast in oblivion, for if Your Most Royal Highness is pleased to give and send me men, I dare venture, therefore, through the goodness of our Lord, to discover very eminent things, and where one can obtain so much gold and enough riches with which to be able to conquer a large part of the world; and if Your Most Royal Majesty is pleased with this and leave me in charge of the things which are necessary to do here, I have so much confidence in the mercy of our Lord that I will know how to give it such proper skill and industry as will bring it all to a good condition and Your Most Royal Highness be well served; and in case that I should not do this, I have no better thing than my head to put in pledge.

So much I certify to Your Most Royal Highness, that I shall seek that which promotes the service of Your Most Royal Highness with more diligence than the Governors who were lost here, Alonso de Ojeda and Diego de Niquesa, for I do not stay in bed while my men go to invade and overrun the country. I must inform Your Most Royal Highness that no company has gone throughout this land, to one part or another, that I have not gone in advance as guide, and even opening the roads with my own hand for those who went with me. . . .

What Must Be Done

Most powerful Lord, as a person who has seen the things of these parts and who has more knowledge of the land than anyone else hitherto has had, and because I desire that the things here which I have commenced may flourish and grow to the state that is best suited to the service of Your Most

A Diversity of Experiences

Complicating perceptions of the accounts left from the European explorers is the fact that they mostly represented a very specific and limited vantage point: that of the male European either of noble birth or seeking to enter the upper classes. In this excerpt from his book Marvelous Possessions, *scholar Stephen Greenblatt recognizes that although testimony representing other perspectives didn't necessarily survive, there would have been many ways of understanding and conceptualizing the New World and its peoples.*

European adventurers . . . were themselves go-betweens, servants of the great representational machine. Journals, letters, memoranda, essays, questionnaires, eyewitness accounts, narrative histories, inventories, legal depositions, theological debates, royal proclamations, official reports, papal bulls, charters, chronicles, notarial records, broadsheets, utopian fantasies, pastoral eclogues, dramatic romances, epic poems—there is in the sixteenth century a flood of textual representation, along with a much smaller production of visual images, that professes to deliver the New World to the Old. . . .

The responses of the natives to the fatal advent of the Europeans survive only in the most fragmentary and problematical form; much of what I would like to learn is forever lost. . . .

It is not only the native Americans whose voices are distorted or unrecorded: if anything, there are even fewer traces of the European lower classes, the common seamen and sol-

Royal Highness, I wish to make known to you what now is proper and necessary to command to be provided, and this is for the present until the land is known and it is found out what is in it.

The principal thing necessary is that one thousand men come from the island Española, for men who now might come from Spain would not be worth much until they would be habituated to the country, because they would perish and we who are here with them. Your Most Royal Highness will have to order that this colony for the present is supplied with

---

diers, the servants and artisans, who endured the greatest hardships and perils of the voyages. Sometimes they are only represented by a number—in casually imprecise remarks like 'som 60 or 70 other soudiars slayn and hurte' or, still less directly, in phrases like 'no one of note was killed or wounded'—sometimes by a simple list of occupations and names. On occasion there is a glimpse of something further, though rarely individuated: a mention of sailors who grumble and threaten to mutiny, or of terrified voices raised in supplication and prayer, or of ferocious, uncontrollable wielders of pikes and swords against naked men and women.

We may tell ourselves that the ordinary seaman and the gentleman adventurer shared the same experiences, and hence that the silence of the former is not especially significant, but there are signs of major differences in perception. When an English serving-woman who had been held captive by the Algonquians reports that her life was hard but no harder than that of a serving-woman at home, or when a Spanish soldier runs away to live with the Mayans and then leads the tribe in attacks against his former countrymen, or when colonists in Virginia establish with the natives illegal trade relations that upset the official rates of exchange, then we are evidently dealing with a different way of construing the otherness of the others than that dominant in the discourse of the European ruling élite.

Stephen Greenblatt, *Marvelous Possessions: The Wonder of the New World.* Chicago: University of Chicago Press, 1991.

provisions by the hand of Your Most Royal Highness. . . .

At the same time there has to be continually provided here many supplies to build small vessels for the rivers [illegible in original] the pitch and nails and sails and more than enough tackle; it is necessary that some masters come who know how to build brigantines: Your Most Royal Highness ought to send two hundred cross-bows made to order, that stays well furnished and the fittings [illegible] and of very strong draw, and that they be no more than up to two pounds, and on them money will be gained, because each one of those here will be glad to have one or two cross-bows; for besides being very good arms against the Indians, they supply many birds and game to men able to possess them. Two dozen very good hand-guns of light metal are needed, because those of iron are soon damaged by the rains and moisture and they are eaten with rust. . . .

For the present, most puissant Lord, on the coming of more men, it is necessary to construct a fortress in the province of Davaibe, the strongest that can be made, because the region is thickly settled with bad people: another fortress must be built among the mines of Tubanamá in the province of Comogre, likewise for the reason that there are many Indians in that territory. . . .

The Slave Trade

The land where the Indians eat men is very poor and unprofitable, and at no time could it be of any benefit: likewise these Indians of the Caribana have well merited death a thousand times, because they are a very wicked people and in other times have killed many Christians . . . I do not say to give them for slaves as being an evil race; better still to command all to be burnt, little and big, in order that no memory might remain of so vile a people: I declare this, Sire, in regard to the point of Caribana [Punta Caribana] and as far as twenty leagues inland, the one because the natives are very bad, and the other for the reason that the land is very sterile and worthless.

It is best that Your Highness give license that all these Indians may be carried to the island Española and to the other islands settled with Christians to be sold and profit from them, and with the price of them other slaves might be brought here; for in order to hold them in these parts [Darien] it is impossible to make use of them, not so much as only one day, because the land is very large where they can run away and hide; so that the Spaniards in these parts not holding Indians secure, it will not be able to do what is conducive to the service of Your Highness, nor can any gold be taken from the mines. . . .

Power Struggles

I do not wish to build castles in the air like those set up by the Governors [Nicuesa and Ojeda] that Your Highness sent here, who between both together lost eight hundred men; and the Spaniards that I have been able to rescue, of those that both left shipwrecked and who escaped, are about fifty, and this is the truth: and Your Highness can see what I have done and discovered, and maintained all these Christians without any aid except that of God and with very great industry, and who has known how to sustain and support himself by the Indians, and it shows by what Your Highness there will see that I will know what to tell him best suits these parts: and if I should err in something that promotes the service of Your Highness, I entreat Your Highness that he accept my most excessive wish and desire to serve Your Highness, and though now, most powerful Lord, I may not comprehend everything that is needed for the future in this land, in the meantime I certify to him that for what is suitable, I will know how to give as good care and skill as all those commanders who until the present have come here; and in order that Your Highness may judge it, behold what the Governors so far appointed have discovered, found out and obtained; for all have gone back lost, and they left here the shores well filled with graves, and even if the many Christians who died might be interred in the ground, the truth is that the greater part of the Christians who died were eaten by dogs and crows: I do not want to lengthen this any more, except to say that by the works Your Highness may see what each one has been able to do and has done until now.

Your Highness must know that in days past there were certain controversies here, because the *Alcaldes* and *Regidores* of this Town, with envy and falsehood, tried to arrest me, and since they could not do it, they made false charges against me and with false witnesses and secretly, of which I complain to Your Highness; for if they should not be punished, never any Governor of those who might come here for Your Highness would fail to have dissensions, for I being *Alcalde Mayor* for Your Highness, they entered against me a thousand iniquities, and have acted in the same manner to all those who have come to these parts; and if the justice of Your Highness is not feared, that which is best for his service never will be done.

And because the *Alcaldes* and *Regidores* transmitted an accusation against me, which I believe Your Highness will see there, I made Judges of two *Hidalgos* in order that they might make an investigation and receive information of my life and of my most loyal and great services that I have performed for Your Highness in these parts of the Indies and main land and these provinces in which now we are, which I send to Your Highness that you may see the wickedness of those people; and because I believe that Your Highness will take much pleasure in all that I have done in his service in these territories, I beg Your Highness to examine it all so that he grant me favors according to my services: I am sending also an information of what happened after they devised their evil deeds.

A Civilization Deemed Worthy of Conquest

Hernán Cortés

For Spaniards such as Hernán Cortés, who could claim a degree of noble blood but lacked secure wealth and prestige, participating in the conquest of the New World offered an opportunity for riches and advancement. Cortés came to Hispaniola (present-day island home of Haiti and the Dominican Republic) in 1504 and served in the conquest of Cuba in 1511. By 1518 the Spanish had sent two expeditions to Yucatan, on the mainland of Mexico, bringing back mixed reports of riches and rumors of an advanced empire.

In 1519, Cortés was chosen to lead another expedition to the mainland, though he was given permission only to pursue limited trade and exploration. Through shrewd and ruthless maneuvering, Cortés disobeyed the orders of his superiors in the New World, instead appealing directly to King Charles V in Spain for authorization of his actual goal: marching inland to the great city of Tenochtitlán (Temixtitan) and conquering Montezuma and his Aztec empire.

In the following letter, the second of five written to Charles, Cortés reveals that his idea of conquest involved establishing a permanent Spanish presence and ruling Mexico as part of a larger Spanish empire, rather than only extracting as much immediate wealth as possible. His strategy for convincing Charles to support his plans relied upon emphasizing the achievements of the Aztec civilization, including their wonderful cities and vast wealth, and illustrating how the Aztec kingdom, when conquered, would be a valuable asset

Hernán Cortés, *Letters of Cortés*, edited and translated by Francis Augustus MacNutt. New York: G.P. Putnam's Sons, 1908.

to the crown. With Montezuma and the Aztecs as loyal subjects, Spain would be able to fully exploit their resources,
increase its own glory (and global reach), and convert millions of natives to Christianity.

In my [first letter], Most Excellent Prince [Charles V of
Spain], I told Your Majesty of all the cities and towns
which until then had offered themselves to your royal service, and which I held subjugated and conquered for you. I
also mentioned that I had information of a great lord called
Montezuma, of whom the natives of this country had told
me, and who lived, according to their computation of distances, about ninety or a hundred leagues from the coast and
port where I had disembarked; and that, confiding in the
greatness of God, and relying on the power of Your Highness's Royal name, I had decided to go and see him, wherever he might be. I even remember that I offered, so far as
this lord was concerned, to accomplish the impossible, for I
vowed to Your Royal Highness, that I would have him prisoner, or dead, or subject to the Royal Crown of Your Majesty.

With this purpose and determination, I left the city of
Cempoal, which I had named Seville, on the sixteenth of
August, with fifteen horsemen, and three hundred foot soldiers, all equipped for war, as best I was able, and as time
permitted. . . .

[One] night I fortified myself in a small tower of their
idols, which stood on a small hill, and afterwards, at daybreak, I left two hundred men and all the artillery in the
camp. As I was the attacking party I went out towards
evening with the horsemen, and a hundred foot soldiers, and
four hundred Indians whom I had brought from Cempoal,
and three hundred from Yztacmastitan. Before the enemy
had time to assemble, I set fire to five or six small places of
about a hundred houses each, and brought away about four
hundred prisoners, both men and women, fighting my way
back to my camp without their doing me harm. At daybreak
the following morning, more than a hundred and forty-nine

thousand men, covering all the country, attacked our camp so determinedly that some of them penetrated into it, rushing about, and thrusting with their swords at the Spaniards. We mustered against them, and Our Lord was pleased so to aid us, that, in about four hours, we managed that they should no more molest us in our camp, although they still kept up some attacks; thus we kept fighting until it grew to be late, when they retired.

The next day I again went out before daybreak, in another direction, without having been observed by the enemy, taking with me the horsemen, a hundred foot-soldiers, and the friendly Indians. I burned more than a hundred villages, one of which had more than three thousand houses, where the villagers fought with me, though there were no other people there. As we carried the banner of the Holy Cross, and were fighting for our Faith, and in the service of Your Sacred Majesty, to Your Royal good fortune God gave us such a victory that we slew many people without our own sustaining any injury. A little after mid-day when the strong force of the people was gathered from parts, we had returned victorious to our camp.

Messengers came from the chiefs the next day, saying that they wished to become vassals of Your Highness and my friends, beseeching me to pardon their past fault; and they brought me provisions, and certain feather-work which they use, and esteem and prize. I answered that they had behaved badly, but that I was satisfied to be their friend, and pardon them for all they had done.

The next day there came about fifty Indians, who, it seemed, were men of some consequence amongst them, saying that they had brought us food, and they went about inspecting the entrances and exits of our camp, and some huts in which we were living. The Cempoalans came and told me to watch them, because they were bad men who had come to spy and see what the damage they could do us, and that I might rest assured they had come for no other purpose. With some dissimulation, I had one of them taken, without being observed by the others, and leading him and the interpreters apart frightened him so that he should tell me the truth. He confessed to me that Sintengal, [Xicotencatl, son of the lord of Titzatlan] the captain-general of this province, was behind one of the hills opposite the camp, with a great number of people, ready to fall upon us that night, for they said that they had tried by day against us, and had gained no advantage, and now they wished to try by night, when their people would fear neither our horses, our cannon, nor our swords; and they had been sent in order to examine our camp, and those points where they could attack us, and how they could burn the straw huts. I at once had another of the said Indians taken, and also asked him, and he confessed the same as the other in the same words, so I took another five or six, and they all agreed in their statements. Seeing this I had all the fifty taken, and cut off their hands, and returned them to their chief, ordering them to say to him, that, by day or night or at any or all times he might come, he would see who we were. I then had my camp fortified as best I could, and posted the people as seemed most suitable, and we rested thus on our guard until sunset.

New Subjects for the King

When it was growing late, our opponents began to descend into two valleys, thinking they were surrounding us secretly, and to get nearer to us for carrying out their intentions. . . .

And so it happened, that when they discovered we were coming with horses to attack them, without stopping or shouting, they fled into some fields of maize, with which the country was almost covered, and lightened themselves of some provisions which they were carrying with them, for the feast they intended to celebrate, if this time they destroyed us entirely. . . .

When we had somewhat rested, I made a sally one night, after having inspected the first watch of the guard, taking a hundred foot, the friendly Indians, and the horsemen; and about a league from our camp five horses and mares fell, unable to go on, so I sent them back. Although those who accompanied me, said that I ought to return, as this was an evil omen, I still pushed ahead, confiding in God's supremacy above everything. Before daybreak I fell upon two towns, in which I slaughtered many people, but I did not want to burn the houses, so as to avoid attracting the attention of other people who were very near. When day dawned I fell upon another large town, which contained according to a count, which I ordered to be taken, more than twenty thousand houses, and, as I had surprised them, I found them unarmed, and the women, and children, running naked through the streets; and we did them some harm. Seeing they could offer no resistance, a certain number of the inhabitants came to beseech me not to do them further injury, for they desired to become vassals of Your Highness, and my friends, and they recognised that they were at fault in not having trusted me, but that henceforth I would see that they would always do what I commanded them in the name of Your Royal Highness, as your very true vassals. Immediately there came to me more than four thousand of them, suing for peace, and they took us out to a fountain where they gave us good food. . . .

A Worthy Conquest

I came to the city [Tlascala], which is about six leagues distant from the dwelling place and camp I had occupied, and is so large and admirable that, although much of what I might say I shall omit, the little which I shall say is almost incredible; for it is much larger than Granada, and very much stronger, having very good buildings, and it contains a great many more people than Granada did when it was taken, and is much better supplied with provisions, such as bread, birds, game, and river-fish, and other good eatables and vegetables. There is a market in this city, in which every day, above thirty thousand souls sell and buy, without counting many other small markets in different parts of the city. Everything is to be found in this market in which they trade, and could need, not only provisions, but also clothing and shoes. There are jewellery shops, for gold, and silver, and stones, and other valuables of feather-work, as well arranged as can be found in any of the squares or market-places of the world;

there is also as good earthenware and crockery as the best in Spain. They also sell wood and coals, and herbs to eat, and for medicinal purposes. There are houses like barbers' shops, where they wash their heads and shave themselves; there are also baths. Finally there prevail good order and politeness, for they are a people full of intelligence and understanding, and such that the best in Africa does not equal them. This province contains many extensive and beautiful valleys, well tilled and sown, and none are uncultivated. The province is ninety leagues in circumference, and, as far as I have been able to judge about the form of government, it is almost like that of [Italian city-states such as] Venice, or Genoa, or Pisa, because there is no one supreme ruler. There are many lords all living in this city, and the people who are tillers of the soil are their vassals, though each one has his lands to himself, some more than others. In undertaking wars, they all gather together, and thus assembled they decide and plan them. It is believed that they must have some system of justice for punishing the wicked. . . . According to the visitation which I ordered to be made, this province has five hundred thousand householders, besides those of another small province, called Guazincango, which joins it, whose people live as these do, without a rightful sovereign, and are no less vassals of Your Highness than these Tascaltecas.

Montezuma's Tribute

Being, Most Catholic Lord, in our camp in the country while I was at warfare with this province, there came to me six lords from amongst the principal vassals of Montezuma, accompanied by about two hundred retainers, telling me that they came on the part of Montezuma to say that he wished to be a vassal of Your Highness, and my friend. He sent word that I should say what I wanted him to give to Your Highness as an annual tribute, of gold, silver, stones, slaves, cotton, and wearing apparel, and other possessions, and that he would give it all, if only I would not come to his country, because it was very sterile, and destitute of provisions, and he would be sorry if I or my people suffered want. He sent me by them about a thousand dollars of gold, and many pieces of cotton clothing, such as they wear. They remained with me during the war and until the end of it, and well saw what the Spaniards were able to do [Cortés ignored the advice and moved on to Tenochtitlán (Temixtitan) to face Montezuma]. . . .

Seizing Montezuma

Six days having passed, Most Invincible Prince, after I had arrived in the city of Temixtitan, and, having seen something of it, although little in proportion to the amount there is to be seen and noted, it appeared to me, even from what I had seen of it and the country, that it would be conducive to Your Royal Highness's service, and to our security, that Montezuma should be in my power, and not at his entire liberty, so that he might not relax his intention and disposition to serve Your Highness. I thought this, especially because we Spaniards are somewhat touchy and importunate, and, if he should happen to become angry, he could do us such injury with his great power, that there would remain no recollection of us; and also because, having him in my power, all the other countries who were subject to him, would come to the knowledge and service of Your Majesty, as afterwards happened.

I determined to seize him, and confine him in my quarters, which are very strong . . .

I will not say more than that finally he agreed to come with me, and [I] immediately gave orders to prepare the apartment he wished to occupy, which was well fitted up, and put in order. This having been done, many lords came, and having taken off their vestments, which they carried under their arms, barefooted they brought the litter, not much adorned, and, weeping, they placed him on it, in profound silence. Thus we went to my quarters without causing any commotion in the city although some had begun, but, when Montezuma heard of it, he ordered it to be stopped. . . .

Montezuma as Vassal

I ordered him to be put in chains, which frightened him not a little. After I had spoken to him, I removed the irons the same day, and he remained very satisfied, and ever afterwards I endeavoured to please him, and keep him satisfied as far as possible; especially did I always say publicly to all the natives of the country, nobles as well as others, who came to see him, that Your Majesty had been pleased that Montezuma should continue to exercise authority, recognising the suzerainty of Your Highness, and that Your Highness would be well pleased by their obeying him, and regarding him as their lord, as they had before I came to the country. So good was my treatment of him, and the satisfaction he felt, that sometimes, and frequently, I offered him his liberty, praying him to return to his palace; but he told me each time that he was contented there, and that he did not wish to go, because nothing that he wished was wanting, more than in his own palace, whereas it might happen that, if he went back, the lords of the country, his vassals, would importune him to do things, in spite of himself, which would be contrary to his own wish, and to Your Highness's service. He added, that he was determined to serve Your Majesty in all that was possible, and up till now he had told them what he wanted done, and was content where he was, for, should anyone attempt to make suggestions to him now, he could excuse himself by answering that he was not free, and thus evade them. . . .

The Search for Gold

When I afterwards understood perfectly, that he was wholly devoted to the service of Your Royal Highness, I prayed him, so that I might give a better account to Your Majesty of this country, to show me the mines from which he obtained gold, and he answered with perfect good will that he would gladly do so. He immediately sent certain of his servants, distributing them two by two over four provinces, from which he said he got the gold; and he asked me to send Spaniards with them, to see how it was taken out. So, for each of his own people, I sent two Spaniards, and some went to a province, called Cuzula, eighty leagues from the great city of Temixtitan, the natives of which are his vassals,

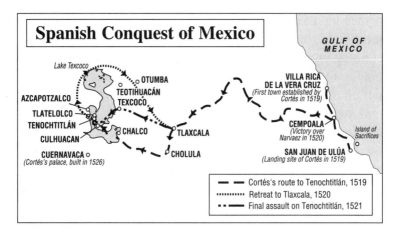

and there they were shown three rivers, from each of which they brought me specimens of gold of very good quality, although it was taken out with mean tools, as they had only those with which the Indians extract it. On the road, they passed through three provinces, according to what the Spaniards said, of fine land, and many hamlets and cities, and towns, very populous, and containing buildings equal to any in Spain. They told me especially of a house and fort, greater, and stronger, and better built, than the castle of Burgos, and that the people of this province, called Tamazulapa, were better dressed than any others we have seen, and, as it seemed to them, more intelligent. Others went to another province called Malinaltepeque, another seventy leagues from the said great city, and more towards the sea-coast; and they brought me likewise specimens of gold from a great river there. . . .

Establishing a Plantation

As there is in those parts, according to what the Spaniards who went there informed me, every facility for making plantations, and procuring gold, I begged Montezuma to establish a plantation for Your Majesty in that province of Malinaltepeque, which seems the best adapted, and he put such diligence into it, that, within two months after I had spoken to him, sixty [bushels] of maize, and ten of beans had been sown, and two thousand plants of [cacao] which bears a fruit somewhat like almonds. This fruit they sell ground, and esteem so highly, that it is used instead of money all over the country, and with it everything can be bought in the market places and elsewhere. He built four good houses, in one of which, besides the living apartments, they made a water tank, and put five hundred ducks in it; these are much esteemed, because they pluck their feathers every year, and use them for making wearing apparel. And they placed fifteen hundred chickens in it, not to speak of other farm stock, which the Spaniards judged to be worth twenty thousand dollars of gold. I also prayed Montezuma to tell me if on the sea-coast there was any river or bay where ships could enter safely, and he answered me that he did not know, but that he would have the coast drawn for me, with its bays and rivers, and that I might send the Spaniards to see them, and that he would give me people to guide and take them; and thus we did. . . .

Almost Like Spain

This great city of Temixtitan is built on the salt lake, and from the mainland to the city is a distance of two leagues, from any side from which you enter. It has four approaches by means of artificial causeways, two cavalry lances in width. The city is as large as Seville or Cordoba. Its streets (I speak of the principal ones) are very broad and straight, some of these, and all the others, are one half land, and the other half water on which they go about in canoes. All the streets have openings at regular intervals, to let the water flow from one to the other, and at all of these openings, some of which are very broad, there are bridges, very large, strong, and well constructed, so that, over many, ten horsemen can ride abreast. . . .

The city has many squares where markets are held, and trading is carried on. There is one square, twice as large as that of Salamanca, all surrounded by arcades, where there are daily more than sixty thousand souls, buying and selling, and where are found all the kinds of merchandise produced in these countries, including food products, jewels of gold and silver, lead, brass, copper, zinc, stone, bones, shells, and feathers. . . .

The people of this city had better manners, and more luxury in their dressing and service, than those of other provinces and cities, for the reason that the sovereign, Montezuma, always resided there, and all the nobles, his vassals, frequented the city, so better manners, and more ceremony prevailed. But to avoid being prolix in describing the things of the city (though I would fain continue), I will not say more than that, in the service and manners of its people, their fashion of living was almost the same as in Spain, with just as much harmony and order; and considering that these people were barbarous, so cut off from the knowledge of God, and other civilised peoples, it is admirable to see to what they attained in every respect. As far as the service surrounding Montezuma is concerned, and the admirable attributes of his greatness and state, there is so much to write that I assure Your Highness I do not know where to begin, so as to finish what I would say of any part respecting it. For, as I have already said, what greater grandeur can there be, than that a barbarian monarch, like him, should have imitations in gold, silver, stones, and feather-work, of all the things existing under heaven in his dominion?—gold, and silver, things, so like to nature, that there is not a silversmith in the world who could do it better; and, respecting the stones, there is no imagination which can divine the instruments with which they were so perfectly executed; and respecting the feather-work, neither in wax, nor in embroidery, could nature be so marvellously imitated.

So far, the extent of Montezuma's kingdom is not known, but everywhere within two hundred leagues on this and the other side of this capital, wherever he sent, his messengers were not disregarded.

Looting the Incan Empire

Francisco de Xeres

Francisco de Xeres accompanied famed Spanish conquistador Francisco Pizarro on his 1532 expedition to Peru. Xeres served as Pizarro's secretary, and wrote the following eyewitness account at his master's request. It was most likely first published in Spain in 1534.

Pizarro had arrived in the New World in 1502, and became a military leader there, accompanying Vasco Núñez de Balboa on his journey across Panama to the Pacific in 1513. He led expeditions to Peru in the 1520s, as the Spaniards were learning more about the vast Incan empire and its leader Atahuallpa (Atabaliba in the following text) and the supposedly unlimited riches available in the largely unexplored interior.

In 1532, although the Incan leader had thousands and thousands of troops at his service, and the Europeans never numbered more than a few hundred, Pizarro successfully ambushed and kidnapped Atahuallpa, holding him hostage as enormous quantities of gold and other treasures—often in the form of artwork and religious icons—were delivered as ransom. These items were melted down for distribution among the conquerors and shipment back to Europe. Thus began the looting of the Incan Empire and its ultimate destruction.

The Governor [Pizarro] said to [a] messenger [from Atahuallpa leader of the Incan empire] . . . :

I would have you to know that my Lord the Emperor

Francisco de Xeres, *Reports on the Discovery of Peru*, translated and edited by Clements R. Markham. New York: Burt Franklin, 1970.

[Charles V], who is King of Spain and of all the Indies and of Tierra Firme [northern South America], and Lord over all the World, has many servants who are greater Lords than Atabaliba [Atahuallpa], and his captains have fought and taken much greater Lords than either Atabaliba, his brother, or his father. The Emperor has sent me to these lands to bring the inhabitants to a knowledge of God, and, in his service, I have defeated greater Lords than Atabaliba, with these few Christians that are with me now. If he should wish for my friendship, and to receive me peacefully, as other Lords have done, I shall be his good friend, and I will assist him in his conquest, leaving him in his present state; for I go through these lands to discover the other sea. . . . I make war upon no one, nor do I molest any one, unless war is made upon me.

When the messengers heard these things, they were at first so astounded that they could not speak, to think that so few Spaniards could have performed such wonderful things. After a time they expressed a wish to go with this reply to their Lord, and to tell him that the Christians would come quickly, in order that he might send out provisions on the road. The Governor dismissed them. The next morning he continued the march, still over the mountains, and that night he slept at some villages he came to, in a valley. As soon as the Governor arrived, there came the chief messenger. . . . The Governor was very glad to see him, and inquired after Atabaliba. The messenger answered that he was well, and that he had sent ten sheep for the Christians. He spoke very freely, and, from his conversation, he seemed to be an intelligent man.

When he had completed his speech, the Governor asked the interpreters what he had said. They answered that he had repeated the same as had been said by the other messengers the day before; but that he had added many arguments, praising the greatness of his Lord and the vast power of his army, and assuring the Governor that Atabaliba would receive him in peace, and that he desired to have him as a friend and a brother. . . .

Atahuallpa Comes in Peace

[Pizarro took his troops to the Incan city of Caxamalca to seek out Atahuallpa. He notified his outnumbered soldiers not to attack the Incas unless they heard the signal cry of "Santiago."] When the Governor saw that it was near sunset, and that Atabaliba did not move from the place to which he had repaired, although troops still kept issuing out of his camp, he sent a Spaniard to ask him to come into the square to see him before it was dark. As soon as the messenger came before Atabaliba, he made an obeisance to him, and made signs that he should come to where the Governor waited. Presently he and his troops began to move, and the Spaniard returned and reported that they were coming, and that the men in front carried arms concealed under their clothes. . . . First came a squadron of Indians dressed in a livery of different colours, like a chess board. They advanced, removing the straws from the ground, and sweeping the road. Next came three squadrons in different dresses, dancing and singing. Then came a number of men with armour, large metal plates, and crowns of gold and silver. Among them was Atabaliba in a litter lined with plumes of macaws' feathers, of many colours, and adorned with plates of gold and silver. Many Indians carried it on their shoulders on high. Next came two other litters and two hammocks, in which were some principal chiefs; and lastly, several squadrons of Indians with crowns of gold and silver.

As soon as the first entered the open space they moved aside and gave space to the others. On reaching the centre of the open space, Atabaliba remained in his litter on high, and the others with him, while his troops did not cease to enter. A captain then came to the front and, ascending the fortress near the open space, where the artillery was posted, raised his lance twice, as for a signal. Seeing this, the Governor asked the Father Friar Vicente if he wished to go and speak to Atabaliba, with an interpreter? He replied that he did wish it, and he advanced, with a cross in one hand and the Bible in the other. . . .

Atabaliba asked for the Book, that he might look at it, and the Priest gave it to him closed. Atabaliba did not know how to open it, and the Priest was extending his arm to do so, when Atabaliba, in great anger, gave him a blow on the arm, not wishing that it should be opened. Then he opened it himself, and, without any astonishment at the letters and paper, as had been shown by other Indians, he threw it away from him five or six paces. . . .

The Slaughter

The Monk [returned and] told the Governor what had passed between him and Atabaliba, and that he had thrown the Scriptures to the ground. Then the Governor put on a jacket of cotton, took his sword and dagger, and, with the Spaniards who were with him, entered amongst the Indians most valiantly; and, with only four men who were able to follow him, he came to the litter where Atabaliba was, and fearlessly seized him by the arm, crying out *Santiago.* Then the guns were fired off, the trumpets were sounded, and the troops, both horse and foot, sallied forth. On seeing the horses charge, many of the Indians who were in the open space fled, and such was the force with which they ran that they broke down part of the wall surrounding it, and many fell over each other. The horsemen rode them down, killing and wounding, and following in pursuit. The infantry made so good an assault upon those that remained that in a short time most of them were put to the sword. The Governor still held Atabaliba by the arm, not being able to pull him out of the litter because he was raised so high. Then the Spaniards made such a slaughter amongst those who carried the litter that they fell to the ground, and, if the Governor had not protected Atabaliba, that proud man would there have paid for all the cruelties he had committed. The Governor, in protecting Atabaliba, received a slight wound in the hand. During the whole time no Indian raised his arms against a Spaniard. So great was the terror of the Indians at seeing the Governor force his way through them, at hearing the fire of the artillery, and beholding the charging of the horses, a thing never before heard of, that they thought more of flying to save their lives than of fighting. All those who bore the litter of Atabaliba appeared to be principal chiefs. They were all killed, as well as those who were carried in the other litters and hammocks. One of them was the page of Atabaliba, and a great lord, and the others were lords of many vassals, and his Councillors. The chief of Caxamalca was also killed, and others; but, the number being very great, no account was taken of them, for all who came in attendance on Atabaliba were great lords. The Governor went to his lodging, with his prisoner Atabaliba, despoiled of his robes, which the Spaniards had torn off in pulling him out of the litter. It was a very wonderful thing to see so great a lord taken prisoner in so short a time, who came in such power. . . .

The battle lasted only about half an hour, for the sun had already set when it commenced. If the night had not come on, few out of the thirty thousand men that came would have been left. It is the opinion of some, who have seen armies in the field, that there were more than forty thousand men. In the square and on the plain there were two thousand killed, besides wounded. . . .

The Spoils

Next morning the Governor sent a Captain, with thirty horse, to scour the plain, and he ordered them to break the arms of the Indians. The troops in the camp made the imprisoned Indians remove the dead bodies from the open space. The Captain, with his horsemen, collected all that was on the plain and in the tents of Atabaliba, and returned to the camp before noon with a troop of men, women, sheep, gold, silver, and cloth. Among these spoils there were eighty thousand *pesos*, seven thousand marcs [a marc was approximately eight ounces] of silver, and fourteen emeralds. The gold and silver were in immense pieces, great and small plates and jars, pots, cups, and other shapes. Atabaliba said that all this was the furniture of his service, and that the Indians who fled had taken a great deal more away with them. . . .

Some [Spaniards] were of opinion that all the Indian soldiers should be killed, or at least, that their hands should be cut off. The Governor would not consent, saying that it would not be well to commit so great a cruelty, for, although the power of Atabaliba was great, and he was able to collect a vast multitude of people, yet the power of our Lord God is, beyond all comparison, greater. . . .

A Hostage

Atabaliba feared that the Spaniards would kill him, so he told the Governor, that he would give his captors a great quantity of gold and silver. The Governor asked him: "How much can you give, and in what time?" Atabaliba said: "I will give gold enough to fill a room twenty-two feet long and seventeen wide, up to a white line which is half way up the wall." The height would be that of a man's stature and a half. He said that, up to that mark, he would fill the room with different kinds of golden vessels, such as jars, pots, vases, besides lumps and other pieces. As for silver, he said he would fill the whole chamber with it twice over. He undertook to do this in two months. The Governor told him to send off messengers with this object, and that, when it was accomplished, he need have no fear. Then Atabaliba sent messages to his captains, who were in the city of Cuzco, ordering them to send two thousand Indians laden with gold and silver. . . .

After some days some of the people of Atabaliba arrived. There was a brother of his, who came from Cuzco, and sisters and wives. The brother brought many vases, jars, and pots of gold, and much silver, and he said that more was on the road; but that, as the journey is so long, the Indians who bring the treasure become tired, and cannot all come so quickly, so that every day more gold and silver will arrive of that which now remains behind. Thus on some days twenty thousand, on others thirty thousand, on others fifty thousand or sixty thousand *pesos* of gold arrived, in vases, great pots weighing two or three *arrobas* [one arroba was approximately twenty-five pounds] and other vessels. The Governor ordered it all to be put in the house where Atabaliba had his guards, until he had accomplished what he had promised. Twenty days of the month of December had passed, when messengers arrived from San Miguel with a letter which informed the Governor that six ships had arrived at the port of Cancebi, near Quaque. . . .

Melting Down the Treasure

The masters of the six ships which were at the port of San Miguel, being unable to maintain their crews, had requested the Governor to pay and despatch them. The Governor called a Council for the purpose of making the necessary arrangements and for reporting what had happened to his Majesty. It was decided that all the gold should be melted down which had been brought to Caxamalca by order of Atabaliba, as well as all that might arrive before the melting was finished. As soon as it was melted and distributed, the Governor would not be detained any longer, but would proceed to form a settlement, in obedience to the orders of his Majesty.

The publication of this resolution and the commencement of the melting took place on the 3rd of May, 1533. After ten days one of three Christians who went to the city of Cuzco arrived. He was the public notary, and he reported that city of Cuzco had been taken possession of in the name of his Majesty. He also gave an account of the road, on which he said there were thirty principal towns, without counting Cuzco, and many other small villages. He said that Cuzco was as large as had been reported, and that it is situated on a hill side near a plain; that the streets were very regularly arranged and paved, and that in the eight days that he had been there he had not been able to see everything. He saw a well-built house entirely plated with gold, quadrangular, and measuring three hundred and fifty paces from corner to corner. Of these gold plates they took down seven hundred, which together weighed 500 *pesos*. From another house the Indians pulled off a quantity weighing 200,000 *pesos;* but, as it was much alloyed, having but seven or eight carats the *peso*, they would not receive it. Besides these two, they did not see any other houses plated with gold; but the Indians did not permit them to see all the city. They judged from what they did see that it was very rich. . . .

[The Spanish captain at Cuzco] calculated that the gold which was on the road would arrive at Caxamalca in about a month. It actually arrived on the 13th of June, and consisted of two hundred loads of gold and twenty-five of silver. The gold appeared to be of more than one hundred and thirty carats. After the arrival of this first instalment another sixty loads of less fine gold came in. The greater part was in plates, like the boards of a box, and three to four *palmos* [one palmo was approximately eight inches] in length. These had been taken from the walls of the house, and they had holes in them, showing that they had been secured by nails. . . . The account was then taken, all being reduced to good gold; and it was found to make a total of 326,539 *pesos* of good gold. After deducting the fees of the founder, the Royal fifth [amount due to the Spanish crown] amounted to 262,259 *pesos* of pure gold. Of the silver there were 51,610 *marcs*, of which 10,121 *marcs* of silver formed the Royal fifth. All the rest, after the Royal fifths and the fees of the founder had been deducted, was divided amongst all the conquerors who accompanied the Governor. . . .

Atahuallpa's "Treason"

Now I must mention a thing which should not be forgotten. A chief, who was Lord of Caxamalca, appeared before the Governor and said to him through the interpreters: "I would have you to know that, after Atabaliba was taken prisoner, he sent to Quito, his native land, and to all the other provinces, with orders to collect troops to march against you and your followers, and to kill you all.". . .

When the Governor heard this, he thanked the chief and did him much honour, and sent for a clerk to put it all down. . . .

Then the Governor, with the concurrence of the officers of his Majesty, and of the captains and persons of experience, sentenced Atabaliba to death. His sentence was that, for the treason he had committed, he should die by burning, unless he became a Christian; and this execution was for the security of the Christians, the good of the whole land, and to secure its conquest and pacification. For on the death of Atabaliba all his troops would presently disperse, and would not have the courage to attack us or to obey his orders.[1] . . .

Pizarro Appoints a New Incan Leader

Soon afterwards the Governor took another son of old Cuzco . . . who had shown a desire to be friendly to the Spaniards, and placed him in the lordship, in presence of the chiefs and lords of the surrounding districts, and of many other Indians. He ordered them to receive him as their lord, and to obey him as they had obeyed Atabaliba; for that he was their proper lord, being legitimate son of old Cuzco. They all answered that they would receive him as their lord, and obey him as the Governor had ordered.

1. The pretext for murdering Atahuallpa was false, and Xeres, the murderer's secretary, knew that it was false when he wrote this narrative.

"Blinded and Dazed" by Greed

Gonzalo Fernández de Oviedo y Valdés

By the late 1530s, countless atrocities had been committed in the New World as conquistadors frantically searched for riches. One such invader was the Spaniard Hernando De Soto, who had participated in the conquests of Costa Rica and Nicaragua, enriched himself with Pizarro in Peru, and in 1537 was appointed governor of Cuba and given the right to conquer "La Florida," a vast and indefinite territory comprising what is now the southern United States.

His expedition into North America included approximately 600 men and lasted four years. De Soto and his army wandered from native settlement to native settlement, occasionally forging alliances but more often fighting running battles and seizing what was needed to avoid starvation. The peoples encountered by De Soto suffered greatly from this contact, ravaged not only through war but also by exposure to European germs and illnesses.

The following extracts are taken from the diary kept by Rodrigo Ranjel, De Soto's private secretary during the expedition. The account surfaced in a larger work by Gonzalo Fernandez de Oviedo y Valdés, who had been appointed "chronicler of the Indies" in 1532, and many of the observations included are clearly those of the historian Oviedo rather than Ranjel. In the account, Oviedo, who opposed Bartolomé de Las Casas's defense of the rights of natives, nevertheless condemns the greed and ruthless violence of the "wicked" invaders.

Gonzalo Fernández de Oviedo y Valdés, *A Narrative of De Soto's Expedition Based on the Diary of Rodrigo Ranjel, His Private Secretary*, edited and translated by Edward Gaylord Bourne. New York: Allerton Book Co., 1922.

This Governor [Hernando De Soto, Spanish governor of Cuba] was much given to the sport of slaying Indians, from the time that he went on military expeditions with the Governor [of the Spanish settlement in Panama] Pedrarias Dávila in the provinces of Castilla del Oro and of Nicaragua; and likewise he was in Peru and present at the capture of that great [Inca] Prince Atabalipa, where he was enriched. He was one of the richest that returned to Spain because he brought to Seville, and put in safe keeping there, upwards of one hundred thousand pesos of gold; and he decided to return to the Indies to lose them with his life and to continue the employment, blood-stained in the past, which he had followed in the countries I mention.

So then, continuing his conquest, he ordered General Vasco Porcallo de Figueroa to go to Oçita [a native village in Florida] because it was reported that people had come together there; and this captain having gone there, he found the people departed and he burned the village and threw an Indian, which he had for a guide, to the dogs. The reader is to understand that *aperrear* (to throw to the dogs), is to have the dogs eat him, or kill him, tearing the Indian in pieces, since the Conquistadores in the Indies have always used to carry Irish greyhounds and very bold, savage dogs. . . .

Kidnapping a Chief

On September 9 [1539] they [the Spaniards] all departed in a body from [the native village of] Aguacaleyquen, taking with them the chief and his daughter, and an Indian of rank named Guatutima as guide, because he professed to know much of the country beyond and gave abundant information. And they made a bridge of pines to cross the river of Aguacaleyquen, and reached a small village for the night. . . . On Friday, September 12, these Christians came to a village which they named Many Waters, because it rained so much that they could not go on either Saturday or Sunday; the Monday following, the 15th, they proceeded and came upon a very bad swamp and all the way was very toilsome, and they slept at Napituca, which is a very pleasant village, in a pretty spot, with plenty of food.

There the Indians employed all their deceptions and devices to recover the chief of Aguacaleyquen, and the affair reached a point that put the Governor in great peril; but their deceptions and tricks were seen through, and he played them a greater one in this fashion. Seven chiefs from the vicinity came together, and sent to say to the Governor that they were subjects of Uçachile, and that by his order and of their own will, they wished to be friends of the Christians and to help them against Apalache, a mighty province hostile to Uçachile and to themselves, and that they had come to him persuaded and requested by Aguacaleyquen (the chief that the Christians had in captivity), and that they were afraid to enter the camp and to be detained; therefore, let the Governor bring Aguacaleyquen with him and go with them to a large plain that was there to negotiate this business. Their dealings were understood, and the message accepted and the Governor went forth to speak with them; but he gave command to the Christians to arm and to mount their horses and at the sound of the trumpet to rush upon the Indians. And having gone to the plain with only his guard and a saddle to sit upon, and accompanied by the chief of Aguacaleyquen, hardly was the Governor seated and the discourse begun, than he saw himself suddenly surrounded with Indians with bows and arrows. From many directions countless others were coming, and immediately the peril was obvious, which the Governor anticipated; and before the trumpet sounded the Master of the Camp, Luis de Moscoso, struck the legs of his horse, shouting "Come on, Knights, Sanctiago, Sanctiago [a code word for "attack"], at them!" And so in a jiffy the cavalry were thrusting many Indians with their lances; and their stratagem was of no use to them and enabled our men to get the start of them in the fighting; yet notwithstanding that they fought like men of great spirit and they killed the Governor's horse and also that of a gentleman named Sagredo, and they wounded others. And after the fighting had lasted a considerable time, the Indians took flight and sought refuge in two ponds; and the Spaniards surrounded one, but the other they could not, and they held that enclosure, watching all the night and until morning, when the Indians surrendered, and they took out from there three hundred and five or six chiefs among them. . . .

Maltreatment

The Indians that were taken in the manner described were carried and put in a wigwam with their hands tied behind their backs; and the Governor went among them to recognize the chiefs, encouraging them in order to induce them to peace and harmony; and he had them released that they might be treated better than the common Indians. One of those chiefs, as they untied him, while the Governor was standing by, threw back his arm and gave the Governor such a tremendous blow that he bathed his teeth in blood and made him spit up much. For this reason they bound him and the others to stakes and shot them with arrows. Other Indians did many other deeds which cannot be fully described, as the historian said, who was present [Rodrigo Ranjel, who served in De Soto's army]. Wherefore, the Governor seeing that the Christians with so few Indians and without arms were so hard pressed, not being less so himself, spoke as follows: "Would to God that those lords of the Council[1] were here to see what it is to serve his majesty in this country!" And it is because they do know it, says the Chronicler [Oviedo], that they have ordered the tyrannies and cruelties to cease, and that the pacification of the Indians shall be carried on in a better way, in order that God our Lord and his Imperial Majesty may be better served, and the consciences of the conquerors be more at peace, and the natives of the country no longer maltreated. . . .

Wandering at Random

On Wednesday, the first of October, the Governor Hernando de Soto, started from Agile and came with his soldiers to the river or swamp of Ivitachuco, and they made a bridge; and

1. The Council of the Indies, established in Spain in 1524 to advise the Spanish crown and supervise Spain's possessions in the New World.

in the high swamp grass on the other side there was an ambuscade of Indians, and they shot three Christians with arrows. They finished crossing this swamp on the Friday following at noon and a horse was drowned there. At nightfall they reached Ivitachuco and found the village in flames, for the Indians had set fire to it. Sunday, October 5, they came to Calahuchi, and two Indians and one Indian woman were taken and a large amount of dried venison. There the guide whom they had ran away. The next day they went on, taking for a guide an old Indian who led them at random, and an Indian woman took them to Iviahica, and they found all the people gone. And the next day two captains went on further and found all the people gone. . . .

Demanding Obedience

This day [in March 1540] they came to a village where some principal Indians appeared as messengers from Ichisi; and one of them addressed the Governor and said three words, one after the other, in this manner: "Who are you, what do you want, where are you going?" And they brought presents of skins, the blankets of the country, which were the first gifts as a sign of peace. All of this took place on Holy Thursday and on the Day of the Incarnation. To the questions of the Indian the Governor replied that he was a captain of the great King of Spain; that in his name he had come to make known to them the holy faith of Christ; that they should acknowledge him and be saved and yield obedience to the Apostolic Church of Rome and to the Supreme Pontiff and Vicar of God, who lived there; and that in temporal affairs they should acknowledge for king and lord the Emperor, King of Castile, our Lord, as his vassals; and that they would treat them well in every thing and that he would maintain toward them peace and justice just the same as towards all his Christian vassals. . . .

"Blinded and Dazed" by Greed

I have wondered many times at the venture-someness, stubbornness, and persistency or firmness, to use a better word for the way these baffled conquerors kept on from one toil to another, and then to another still greater; from one danger to many others, here losing one companion, there three and again still more, going from bad to worse without learning by experience. Oh, wonderful God! that they should have been so blinded and dazed by a greed so uncertain and by such vain discourses as Hernando de Soto was able to utter to those deluded soldiers, whom he brought to a land where he had never been, nor put foot into, and where three other leaders, more experienced than he, had ruined themselves. . . .

Lost in a Labyrinth

The Christians now were without provisions and with great labour they crossed this river and reached some huts of fishermen or hunters. And the Indians whom they carried had now lost their bearings and no longer knew the way; nor did the Spaniards know it, or in what direction they should go; and among them were divers opinions. Some said they should turn back; others said they ought to go on in a different direction; and the Governor proposed, as he always had done, that it was best to go on, without knowing, either himself or they, what they were aiming at or whither they were wandering. And being at a loss in this labyrinth, on Friday, the 23d of April, the Governor sent to look for roads or villages in the following manner: Baltasar de Gallegos was to go up the river northwest, and Johan de Añasco was to go along the river southeast, each with ten horsemen and rations of ten days. And on that day other captains returned from searching and they had found nothing. . . . And so as best they could they supplied their needs, not without great struggle and toil, the horses without any food; they and their masters dying of hunger; with no trail, drenched with continual rain, the rivers always rising and narrowing the land, and without hope of villages or knowledge where to find them, lamenting and calling on God for mercy. . . .

The next day, Friday [May 21, 1540], they were at Xuala,[2]

2. Most likely in northern Georgia or western North Carolina.

which is a village in a plain between two rivers, and the chief was so prosperous that he gave the Christians whatever they asked—tamemes [native servants serving as porters], corn, dogs, *petacas*, and as much as he had. *Petacas* are baskets covered with leather and likewise ready to be so covered with their lids, for carrying clothes or whatever they want to. . . . In that Xuala region it seemed that there were more indications that there were gold mines than in all the country they had traversed and viewed in that northern region. . . .

"Oh, Wicked Men!"

The historian asked a very intelligent gentleman who was with this Governor, and who went with him through his whole expedition in this northern country, why, at every place they came to, this Governor and his army asked for those tamemes or Indian carriers, and why they took so many women and these not old nor the most ugly; and why, after having given them what they had, they held the chiefs and principal men; and why they never tarried nor settled in any region they came to, adding that such a course was not settlement or conquest, but rather disturbing and ravaging the land and depriving the natives of their liberty without converting or making a single Indian either a Christian or a friend. He replied and said: That they took these carriers or tamemes to keep them as slaves or servants to carry the loads of supplies which they secured by plunder or gift, and that some died, and others ran away or were tired out, so that it was necessary to replenish their numbers and to take more; and the women they desired both as servants and for their foul uses and lewdness, and that they had them baptized more on account of carnal intercourse with them than to teach them the faith; and that if they held the chiefs and principal men captive, it was because it would keep their subjects quiet, so that they would not molest them when foraging or doing what they wished in their country; and that whither they were going neither the Governor nor the others knew, but that his purpose was to find some land rich enough to satiate his greed and to get knowledge of the great secrets this Governor said he had heard in regard to those regions according to much information he had received; and as for stirring up the country and not settling it, nothing else could be done until they found a site that was satisfactory.

Oh, wicked men! Oh, devilish greed! Oh, bad consciences! Oh, unfortunate soldiers! that ye should not have understood the perils ye were to encounter, and how wasted would be your lives, and without rest your souls!

Chapter 4

Inland Journeys

Chapter Preface

In the decades following the initial European discovery of the "West Indies" and the Americas, countless expeditions were launched into the interiors of these regions. The stated goals were often the same that drove the initial voyages: to find an easier water passage to Asia, to spread the word of Christianity, and to discover new sources of wealth. Especially regarding the latter motivation, the role of legend and myth came to provide a major catalyst.

In South America, for example, rumors spread of a golden empire so wealthy that the king covered himself with fresh gold dust every day rather than simply wear gold adornments like other kings. This legend of "El Dorado" compelled many to seek their fortunes in exploring the interior. From one such expedition launched from Quito (in modern-day Ecuador), Spanish soldier and explorer Francisco Orellana's smaller party departed and explored the Amazon River. Although Orellana did not find El Dorado, he did claim to have encountered a mythical tribe of women warriors known as the Amazons. Expeditions such as those of Orellana hoped to discover the type of empires already being looted and destroyed in Peru and Mexico.

Much farther north, one of the few survivors of a 1528 expedition to Florida was Álvar Núñez Cabeza de Vaca, who completed his incredible walking journey of survival across what is now the southwestern United States and into Mexico. His tales of adventure hinted at the existence of inland kingdoms of advanced civilization and great wealth. One of the myths of the Old World—of an island in the Atlantic called Antilia, upon which lay the rich and wondrous Seven Cities of Cibola—was transplanted to the New World. Expeditions such as those of Francisco Vásquez de Coronado, who explored from 1540 to 1542 what would become the southwest United States, thus made finding the fantastic cities of Cibola their goal.

The legend of Cibola was not the only myth inspiring the settlers and conquerors. For example, the Spanish had also heard about another wonderfully developed and rich kingdom in the interior of North America: Quivira. Later explorers such as Juan de Oñate made it to Quivira, or present-day western Kansas, and found little but natives who were growing increasingly less tolerant of European invasions. Additionally, Europeans in the New World had heard that the Caribbean natives believed in the existence of a magical spring that had the power to restore youth to those that drank of it; legends and historical accounts romantically assert that this was one of the main goals of Juan Ponce de León in his expedition of exploration and conquest in Florida in 1512.

The Wondrous Cities of the Aztecs

Bernal Díaz del Castillo

> Bernal Díaz del Castillo was a Spanish soldier and chronicler
> who arrived in the New World in 1514 and participated in
> three expeditions launched into Mexico from the Spanish
> bases in Cuba. The third expedition, headed by Hernán Cortés
> and begun in 1519, resulted in the death of the Aztec leader
> Montezuma, the destruction of his marvelous capital city,
> Tenochtitlán (referred to by Díaz as the "City of Mexico"),
> and the fall of the Aztec empire. Díaz was not a particularly
> noted soldier, but was more recognized for his account of the
> conquest, which he wrote back in Spain in the 1560s, many
> decades after the events themselves.
>
> Debates about the actions of Spanish conquistadors in the
> New World were well under way by the time Díaz wrote this
> account, and his approach was much more favorable to Cortés
> than those of others, such as Bartolomé de Las Casas, who was
> harshly critical of those who would kill and enslave the natives
> in a search for riches and power. In the following passages,
> Díaz tells of Montezuma's attempts to prevent the Spanish
> advance and the reception of Cortés by Montezuma in
> Tenochtitlán. Further, he describes the stunning sights the army
> saw while conquering the Aztecs, a people who had constructed
> remarkable cities and a powerful and advanced civilization.

One morning we started on our march to the city of
Cholula [southeast of Tenochtitlán] and we took the

Bernal Díaz del Castillo, *The True History of the Conquest of New Spain*, edited by Genaro
Garcia, translated by Alfred Percival Maudslay. Nendeln, Liechtenstein: Kraus Reprint
Limited, 1967.

greatest possible precautions, for as I have often said, where we expected to encounter tumults or wars we were much more on the alert.

That day we went on to sleep at a river which runs within a short league of Cholula, where there is now a stone bridge, and there they put up for us some huts and ranchos. This same night the Caciques [chiefs] of Cholula sent some chieftains to bid us welcome to their country, and they brought supplies of poultry and maize bread, and said that in the morning all the Caciques and priests would come out to receive us, and they asked us to forgive their not having come sooner. Cortés told them through our interpreters Doña Marina and Jerónimo de Aguilar, that he thanked them both for the food they had brought and for the good will which they showed us. . . .

Cortés's Warning

Then Cortés began to make a speech to them, saying that our Lord and King [Charles V of Spain], whose vassals we were, had very great power and held beneath his sway many great princes and Caciques, and that he had sent us to these countries to give them warning, and command them not to worship Idols, nor sacrifice human beings, or eat their flesh, or practice sodomy or other uncleanness, and as the road to Mexico, whither we were going to speak with the Great Montezuma, passed by there, and there was no other shorter road, we had come to visit their city and to treat them as brothers. As other great Caciques had given their obedience to His Majesty, it would be well that they should give theirs as the others had done. . . .

Montezuma's Entreaty

As we were starting on our march to Mexico there came before Cortés four Mexican chiefs sent by Montezuma who brought a present of gold and cloths. After they had made obeisance according to their custom, they said—"Malinche,[1]

---

1. Used here as a form of address for Cortés but also another name for Doña Marina, Cortés's native translator.

our Lord the Great Montezuma sends you this present and says that he is greatly concerned for the hardships you have endured in coming from such a distant land in order to see him, and that he has already sent to tell you that he will give you much gold and silver and chalchihuites [emerald stones] as tribute for your Emperor and for yourself and the other Teules[2] in your company, provided you will not come to Mexico, and now again he begs as a favour, that you will not advance any further but return whence you have come, and he promises to send you to the port a great quantity of gold and silver and rich stones for that King of yours, and, as for you, he will give you four loads of gold and for each of your brothers one load, but as for going on to Mexico your entrance into it is forbidden, for all his vassals have risen in arms to prevent your entry, and besides this there is no road thither, only a very narrow one, and there is no food for you to eat." And he used many other arguments about the difficulties to the end that we should advance no further. . . .

Cortés answered them that he marvelled how the Lord Montezuma, having given himself out as our friend, and being such a great Prince, should be so inconstant; that one time he says one thing and another time sends to order the contrary, and regarding what he says about giving gold to our Lord the Emperor and to ourselves, he is grateful to him for it, and what he sends him now he will pay for in good works as time goes on. How can he deem it befitting that being so near to his city, we should think it right to return on our road without carrying through what our Prince has commanded us to do? If the Lord Montezuma had sent his messengers and ambassadors to some great prince such as he is himself, and if, after nearly reaching his house, those messengers whom he sent should turn back without speaking to the Prince about that which they were sent to say, when they came back into his [Montezuma's] presence with such a story, what favour would he show them? He would merely treat them as cowards of little worth; and this is what our

2. An Aztec word meaning "idols" but also applied to the seemingly divine Spaniards.

Emperor would do with us, so that in one way or another we were determined to enter his city, and from this time forth he must not send any more excuses on the subject, for he [Cortés] was bound to see him, and talk to him and explain the whole purpose for which we had come, and this he must do to him personally. . . .

Amazing Cities

The next day, in the morning, we arrived at a broad Causeway [a raised road or path], and continued our march towards Iztapalapa, and when we saw so many cities and villages built in the water and other great towns on dry land and that straight and level causeway going towards Mexico, we were amazed and said that it was like the enchantments they tell of in the legend of Amadis [chivalric hero of a fifteenth-century Spanish romance], on account of the great towers and cues and buildings rising from the water, and all built of masonry. And some of our soldiers even asked whether the things that we saw were not a dream? It is not to be wondered at that I here write it down in this manner, for there is so much to think over that I do not know how to describe it, seeing things as we did that had never been heard of or seen before, not even dreamed about.

Thus, we arrived near Iztapalapa, to behold the splendour of the other Caciques who came out to meet us, who were the Lord of the town named Cuitlahuac, and the Lord of Culuacan, both of them near relations of Montezuma. And then when we entered that city of Iztapalapa, the appearance of the palaces in which they lodged us! How spacious and well built they were, of beautiful stone work and cedar wood, and the wood of other sweet scented trees, with great rooms and courts, wonderful to behold, covered with awnings of cotton cloth.

When we had looked well at all of this, we went to the orchard and garden, which was such a wonderful thing to see and walk in, that I was never tired of looking at the diversity of the trees, and noting the scent which each one had, and the paths full of roses and flowers, and the many fruit trees and native roses, and the pond of fresh water. There was another thing to observe, that great canoes were able to pass into the garden from the lake through an opening that had been made so that there was no need for their occupants to land. And all was cemented and very splendid with many kinds of stone [monuments] with pictures on them, which gave much to think about. Then the birds of many kinds and breeds which came into the pond. I say again that I stood looking at it and thought that never in the world would there be discovered other lands such as these, for at that time there was no Peru [explored and conquered by Francisco Pizzaro in the 1530s] nor any thought of it. [Of

A Native Perspective of the Conquest

Although many firsthand accounts of the European discovery and conquest of the New World are available from European authors such as Bernal Díaz del Castillo, writings and oral histories of the original inhabitants are less accessible and rarely studied. The following chronicle and lament describes a battle between the invading forces of Hernán Cortés and people from Tlatelolco, a part of the Aztec city of Tenochtitlán. While it is not certain who was the actual author, the account was written in the indigenous Nahuatl language in 1528, only a few years after Cortés's conquest.

A nd all these misfortunes befell us. We saw them and wondered at them; we suffered this unhappy fate.

Broken spears lie in the roads;
we have torn our hair in our grief.
The houses are roofless now, and their walls
are red with blood.

Worms are swarming in the streets and plazas,
and the walls are splattered with gore.
The water has turned red, as if it were dyed,
and when we drink it,
it has the taste of brine.

all these wonders that I then beheld] to-day all is overthrown and lost, nothing left standing. . . .

The City of Mexico

Early next day we left Iztapalapa with a large escort of those great Caciques whom I have already mentioned. We proceeded along the Causeway which is here eight paces in width and runs so straight to the City of Mexico that it does not seem to me to turn either much or little, but, broad as it is, it was so crowded with people that there was hardly room for them all, some of them going to and others returning from Mexico, besides those who had come out to see us, so

We have pounded our hands in despair
against the adobe walls,
for our inheritance, our city, is lost and dead.
The shields of our warriors were its defense,
but they could not save it.

We have chewed dry twigs and salt grasses;
we have filled our mouths with dust and bits of adobe;
we have eaten lizards, rats and worms. . . .

When we had meat, we ate it almost raw. It was scarcely on the fire before we snatched it and gobbled it down.

They set a price on all of us: on the young men, the priests, the boys and girls. The price of a poor man was only two handfuls of corn, or ten cakes made from mosses or twenty cakes of salty couch-grass. Gold, jade, rich cloths, quetzal feathers—everything that once was precious was now considered worthless.

The captains delivered several prisoners of war to Cuauhtemoc [Aztec successor to Montezuma] to be sacrificed. He performed the sacrifices in person, cutting them open with a stone knife.

Miguel Leon-Portilla, ed., *The Broken Spears: The Aztec Account of the Conquest of Mexico*. Translated from Nahuatl into Spanish by Angel Maria Garibay K. English translation by Lysander Kemp. Boston: Beacon, 1962.

that we were hardly able to pass by the crowds of them that came; and the towers and cues were full of people as well as the canoes from all parts of the lake. It was not to be wondered at, for they had never before seen horses or men such as we are.

Gazing on such wonderful sights, we did not know what to say, or whether what appeared before us was real, for on one side, on the land, there were great cities, and in the lake ever so many more, and the lake itself was crowded with canoes, and in the Causeway were many bridges at intervals, and in front of us stood the great City of Mexico, and we,— we did not even number four hundred soldiers! And we well remembered the words and warnings given us by the people of Huexotzingo and Tlaxcala and Tlamanalco, and the many other warnings that had been given that we should beware of entering Mexico, where they would kill us, as soon as they had us inside.

Let the curious readers consider whether there is not much to ponder over in this that I am writing. What men have there been in the world who have shown such daring? But let us get on, and march along the Causeway. When we arrived where another small causeway branches off (leading to Coyoacan, which is another city) where there were some buildings like towers, which are their oratories [places of prayer], many more chieftains and Caciques approached clad in very rich mantles, the brilliant liveries of one chieftain differing from those of another, and the causeways were crowded with them. The Great Montezuma had sent these great Caciques in advance to receive us, and when they came before Cortés they bade us welcome in their language, and as a sign of peace, they touched their hands against the ground, and kissed the ground with the hand.

Montezuma Arrives

There we halted for a good while, and Cacamatzin, the Lord of Texcoco, and the Lord of Iztapalapa and the Lord of Tacuba and the Lord of Coyoacan went on in advance to meet the Great Montezuma, who was approaching in a rich litter accompanied by other great Lords and Caciques, who owned vassals. When we arrived near to Mexico, where there were some other small towers, the Great Montezuma got down from his litter, and those great Caciques supported him with their arms beneath a marvellously rich canopy of green coloured feathers with much gold and silver embroidery and with pearls and chalchihuites suspended from a sort of bordering, which was wonderful to look at. The Great Montezuma was richly attired according to his usage, and he was shod with sandals . . . the soles were of gold and the upper part adorned with precious stones. The four Chieftains who supported his arms were also richly clothed according to their usage, in garments which were apparently held ready for them on the road to enable them to accompany their prince, for they did not appear in such attire when they came to receive us. Besides these four Chieftains, there were four other great Caciques, who supported the canopy over their heads, and many other Lords who walked before the Great Montezuma, sweeping the ground where he would tread and spreading cloths on it, so that he should not tread on the earth. Not one of these chieftains dared even to think of looking him in the face, but kept their eyes lowered with great reverence, except those four relations, his nephews, who supported him with their arms.

Montezuma Greets the Invaders

When Cortés was told that the Great Montezuma was approaching, and he saw him coming, he dismounted from his horse, and when he was near Montezuma, they simultaneously paid great reverence to one another. Montezuma bade him welcome and our Cortés replied through Doña Marina wishing him very good health. And it seems to me that Cortés, through Doña Marina, offered him his right hand, and Montezuma did not wish to take it, but he did give his hand to Cortés and then Cortés brought out a necklace which he had ready at hand, made of glass stones, which I have already said are called Margaritas, which have within them many patterns of diverse colours, these were strung on a cord of gold and with musk so that it should have a sweet scent, and he placed it round the neck of the Great Montezuma and when he had so placed it he was going to embrace him, and those great Princes who accompained Montezuma held back Cortés by the arm so that he should not embrace him, for they considered it an indignity. . . .

Then Montezuma spoke other words of politeness to him, and told two of his nephews who supported his arms, the Lord of Texcoco and the Lord of Coyoacan, to go with us and show us to our quarters, and Montezuma with his other two relations, the Lord of Cuitlahuac and the Lord of Tacuba who accompanied him, returned to the city, and all those grand companies of Caciques and chieftains who had come with him returned in his train. As they turned back after their Prince we stood watching them and observed how they all marched with their eyes fixed on the ground without looking at him, keeping close to the wall, following him with great reverence. Thus space was made for us to enter the streets of Mexico, without being so much crowded. But who could now count the multitude of men and women and boys who were in the streets and on the azoteas, and in canoes on the canals, who had come out to see us. It was indeed wonderful, and, now that I am writing about it, it all comes before my eyes as though it had happened but yesterday. Coming to think it over it seems to be a great mercy that our Lord Jesus Christ was pleased to give us grace and courage to dare to enter into such a city.

Traveling with the Indians

Álvar Núñez Cabeza de Vaca

Álvar Núñez Cabeza de Vaca was from a respected Spanish
military family. After serving in Europe, he joined the 1528
expedition of Pánfilo de Narváez to the unexplored and vast
territory stretching from eastern Mexico to Florida. After
seven months of exposure to the elements, starvation, and battles with Indians, what remained of the force that had landed
on the coast of Florida tried a risky raft voyage across the
gulf to Mexico. Fewer than a hundred survivors washed up on
the shore of an island off the coast of Texas, and this number
dwindled steadily. Cabeza de Vaca spent years among local
Indians, until he was reunited with three other survivors
around 1533. They then began a journey across Texas and
Mexico and arrived at a Spanish outpost in 1536. They later
moved on to Mexico City, having walked several thousand
miles across the continent.

The account that follows was published in 1555. It is
remarkable for its descriptions of an incredible undertaking
that revealed the size of the new continent and the nature of
its climate, geography, and inhabitants. It is also striking for
the outlook its author developed regarding the Indians, whose
language he learned, food he shared, and customs he tried to
understand. By the time he and his companions finally completed their crossing, Cabeza de Vaca's outlook had changed,
and the way he describes the Spaniards they encountered
indicates that he no longer identified entirely with the conquerors of the New World.

Álvar Núñez Cabeza de Vaca, *The Account: Álvar Núñez Cabeza de Vaca's* Relación,
translated by Martin A. Favata and José B. Fernández. Houston: Arte Público, 1993. Copyright © 1993 by Arte Público Press. Reproduced by permission.

I had to stay with these same Indians from the island [present-day Galveston Islands off the southeast coast of Texas] for over a year. Because they worked me so hard and treated me so poorly, I decided to flee from them and go to those that live in the forests and mainland, a people called the Charruco. I could not bear the kind of life I had with them. Among many other afflictions, in order to eat I had to pull the roots from the ground under the water among the canes where they grew. My fingers were so worn by this that a light brush with a piece of straw would cause them to bleed. And the canes cut me in many places because many of them were broken and I had to go among them with the clothing that I have said I was wearing. For this reason I went over to the other Indians and fared a bit better with them. I became a trader and tried to ply my trade the best I could. Because of this they fed me and treated me well, asking me to go from one place to another for things they needed, since people do not travel or trade much in that land because of the continuous warfare that goes on. . . .

More Survivors

We saw some Indians who came to see our Indians and told us that farther ahead there were three men like us and gave us their names. When we asked them about the other men, they replied that all had died of cold and starvation and that the Indians up ahead had killed Diego Dorantes, Valdivieso and Diego de Huelva for sport when the men went from one lodge to another. They also said that other Indians, their neighbors, had killed Esquivel and Méndez because of a dream they had, and that Captain Dorantes was now with them. We inquired about the condition of the surviving men. They told us that they were mistreated very much, because boys and other Indians among them, that are very lazy and mean, kicked and slapped them, and beat them with sticks. Such was the kind of life they led among them.

We inquired about the land ahead and what was in it to sustain us. They replied that it was very sparsely populated, with no food, and a place where people died of exposure to the cold, since they had no hides or other coverings. . . .

[Cabeza de Vaca met up with the three Spaniards—Alonso del Castillo, Andrés Dorantes, and Figueroa—two days later. Figueroa related—second-hand—the fate of other members of the expedition.] Figueroa said that he learned from Esquivel what had happened to the Governor[1] and the Purser and the others. Esquivel told him that the Purser and the friars had run their boat aground between the rivers. While the Governor's boat was proceeding along the coast, he and his men landed, and the Governor continued on with his boat until he arrived at that large inlet. From there he turned back to board the men and take them to the other side, and he returned for the Purser and the friars and all the others. He said that, once they disembarked, the Governor revoked the Purser's commission to be his lieutenant, and reassigned it to a captain named Pantoja who had come with him. Figueroa also said that the Governor stayed in his boat that night and did not want to go ashore. A sailing master and a sick page stayed with him, but there was no food or water on the boat. At midnight the north wind blew so strongly that it carried the boat out to sea, since it had only a stone anchor, without anyone seeing it. That was the last they heard of him. When they saw what had happened, those who were on land went along the coast. Hindered by a large body of water, they built rafts with great difficulty and crossed to the other side on them. Moving on, they arrived at the edge of a wood on the shore. There they found Indians who, when they saw them coming, put their lodges in their canoes and crossed to the other side of the coast. And the Christians, seeing what the weather was like, since it was November, stayed in these woods where they found water and firewood and some crabs and shellfish, and where little by little they began to die of cold and hunger.

Moreover, Pantoja, who was now in charge, treated them badly. Sotomayor, brother of Vasco Porcallo from the island of Cuba, who had sailed with the fleet as a Senior Officer

1. Pánfilo de Narváez, leader of the original expedition who had been granted the right to colonize the land from eastern Mexico to Florida

of the Militia, and unable to bear it any longer, had a fight with Pantoja and dealt him a heavy blow that killed him on the spot. And so there were fewer and fewer of them. As the men died, the survivors cut and dried their flesh. The last one to die was Sotomayor, and Esquivel cut and dried his flesh, surviving by eating it until the first of March, when an Indian who had fled there came to see if they had died and took Esquivel away with him. While Esquivel was held by this Indian, Figueroa talked to him and found out everything we have just related. . . .

Among the Indians

Some Indians came to Castillo telling him that their heads hurt a great deal, and begging him to cure them. After he made the sign of the cross on them and commended them to God, they immediately said that all their pain was gone. They went to their lodges and brought many prickly pears and a piece of venison, which we did not recognize. Since news of this spread among them, many other sick people came to him that night to be healed. . . .

Throughout the land the only thing people talked about was the marvelous deeds that God our Lord worked through us, and people came from many places asking us to cure them. . . .

Our fame spread throughout the area, and all the Indians who heard about it came looking for us so that we could cure them and bless their children. When the Cutalchiches, the people who were with our Indians, had to leave for their homeland, they offered us all the prickly pears they had stored for their journey, without keeping any. They gave us flints up to a palm and a half long, which they use for cutting and which they highly prize. They asked us to remember them and to pray to God for their good health, and we promised them that we would. With this they left as the happiest people in the world, after giving us the best things they had.

A Growing Sympathy

We remained with those Avavares Indians for eight months, keeping track of the time by the phases of the moon. . . .

None of these peoples reckoned time by the sun or the moon, nor did they keep track of the month or the year. But they do understand and know about the different seasons when fruits ripen or fish die. They are very skilled and practiced in knowing when stars appear. We were always treated well by these people, although we had to dig for our food and carry our share of water and firewood. Their dwellings and foods are like those of the previous groups we encountered, although they suffer more hunger because they have no corn, acorns or nuts. We always walked around nude with them, covering ourselves at night with deerskins. We were very hungry for six of the eight months we spent with them. Another thing they lack is fish. . . .

I traded with these Indians, in bows and arrows and nets and made combs for them. We made mats, which they need very much. Even though they know how to make them, they do not want to be occupied in doing other things because they have to search for food instead. When they work on them, they suffer a great deal from hunger. At other times they would tell me to scrape and soften skins. I was never better off than the days they gave me skins to scrape, because I would scrape them very well and eat the scrapings, which was enough to sustain me for two or three days. It also happened that when these people, or the ones we were with before, gave us a piece of meat, we ate it raw, because if we tried to roast it, the first Indian that came by would take it and eat it. We thought that we should not risk losing the piece of meat. Besides, we were in no condition to take the trouble to eat it roasted, since we could better digest it raw. Such was the life we led there. What little food we had we earned from the trinkets we made with our own hands. . . .

Fear of Christians

At this time Castillo saw a buckle from a sword belt around an Indian's neck, with a horseshoe nail sewn to it. Castillo took it away from him and we asked the Indian what it was. They replied that it had come from heaven. We questioned them further, asking them who had brought it from there.

They told us that some bearded men like us, with horses, lances and swords, had come there from heaven and gone to that river and had speared two Indians. . . .

We traveled far and found the entire country empty because the people who lived there were fleeing into the mountains, not daring to work the fields or plant crops for fear of the Christians. It was very pitiful for us to see such a fertile and beautiful land, filled with water and rivers, with abandoned and burned villages, and to see that the people, who were weakened and sick, all had to flee and hide. Since they could not plant crops, they were very hungry and had to survive by eating tree bark and roots. We too had to endure this hunger all along this route, since they were so miserable that they looked as though they were about to die and could hardly be expected to provide much for us. They brought us blankets that they had hidden from the Christians and gave them to us. They told us how on different occasions the Christians had raided their land and had destroyed and burned villages and carried off half the men and all the women and children. Those who had been able to escape from their clutches were fleeing. We saw that they were so terrorized that they did not dare to stay in one place. They could not plant or cultivate their fields. They were determined to die and thought this would be better than to wait for such cruel treatment as they had already received. They were very pleased to see us, but we feared that when we reached the Indians who lived on the border with Christians and were at war with them, those people would mistreat us and make us pay for what the Christians were doing to them. But since God our Lord was pleased to bring us to them, they began to be in awe of us and revere us as the previous people had done, and even more so, which amazed us. By this, one can clearly recognize that all these people, in order to be attracted to becoming Christians and subjects of your Imperial Majesty, need to be treated well; this is a very sure way to accomplish this; indeed, there is no other way. . . .

After we clearly saw traces of Christians and realized that we were so near them, we gave great thanks to God our

Lord for willing that we should be brought out of our sad and wretched captivity. Anyone considering the length of time we spent in that land and the dangers and afflictions we suffered can imagine the delight we felt. . . . The following morning I caught up with four Christians on horseback who were quite perturbed to see me so strangely dressed and in the company of Indians. They looked at me for a long time, so astonished that they were not able to speak or ask me questions. I told them to take me to their captain. So we went to a place half a league from there, where Diego de Alcaraz, their captain, was. After I spoke to him, he told me that he had quite a problem because he had not been able to capture Indians for many days. . . .

Quarrels Among Christians

After this we had many great quarrels with the Christians because they wanted to enslave the Indians we had brought with us. We were so angry that when we departed we left many Turkish-style bows that we were carrying, as well as many pouches and arrows, among them the five with the emeralds, which we lost because we forgot about them. We gave the Christians many buffalo-hide blankets and other things we had. We had great difficulty in persuading the Indians to return to their homes, to feel secure and to plant corn. They wanted only to accompany us until they handed us over to other Indians, as was their custom. They feared that if they returned without doing this they would die, but they did not fear the Christians or their lances when they were with us. The Christians did not like this and had their interpreter tell them that we were the same kind of people they were, who had gotten lost a long time before, and that we were people of little luck and valor. They said that they were the lords of that land, and that the Indians should obey and serve them, but the Indians believed very little or nothing of what they were saying. Speaking among themselves, they said instead that the Christians were lying, because we had come from the East and they had come from the West; that we healed the sick and they killed the healthy; that we were naked and barefooted and they were dressed and on horseback, with lances; that we coveted nothing but instead gave away everything that was given to us and kept none of it, while the sole purpose of the others was to steal everything they found, never giving anything to anybody. In this manner they talked about us, praising everything about us and saying the contrary about the others. . . .

When the Indians departed they told us that they would do what we said and would settle their villages if the Christians would allow them. I want to make it quite clear and certain that if they should not do so, the Christians will be to blame. After we sent the Indians away in peace, thanking them for the trouble they had taken with us, the Christians sent us under guard to a certain Justice named Cebreros and two other men with him, who took us through wilderness and uninhabited areas to keep us from talking to Indians and so that we could not see or understand what they really did to the Indians. From this, one can see how easily the ideas of men are thwarted, for we wanted freedom for the Indians, and when we thought we had secured it, quite the opposite happened, since the Christians had planned to attack the Indians whom we had reassured and sent in peace. They carried out their plan.

Negotiating on the St. Lawrence

Jacques Cartier

Jacques Cartier was a French sailor who had risen to the title of "master pilot," and in 1534 was the choice of King Francis I to lead an expedition building on the success of an earlier journey to North America by Giovanni da Verrazzano. The goal, as with so many other explorations, was to find new sources of riches and perhaps a northern sea route to Asia.

Cartier led two expeditions to the Newfoundland region and accompanied a third. The accounts of the three voyages, from which the following passages are taken, were published in the sixteenth century; it is not certain that Cartier himself wrote them but they were most likely based on logs he kept. As he learned, the St. Lawrence River was not the elusive and much sought after passage to Asia; nor could he find the wealthy fabled kingdom of Saguenay. Yet Cartier's experiences illustrate much about the realities of inland exploration. Most important were difficulties in communication, as the Europeans and natives tried to understand one another despite language and cultural barriers. As becomes clear in these accounts, relationships that began in friendship could rapidly become tainted with distrust and animosity. Before departing for home at the end of the second voyage, Cartier kidnapped several Iroquois Indians, including a chief, in order to present them to the French court to testify to the wealth and wonders of the New World. The Indians did not survive to return from France.

On [Friday] the twenty-fourth of the said month [July 1534], we had a cross made thirty feet high, which was put together in the presence of a number of savages on the point at the entrance to this harbour,[1] under the crossbar of which we fixed a shield with three *fleurs-de-lys* in relief, and above it a wooden board, engraved in large Gothic characters, where was written, LONG LIVE THE KING OF FRANCE. We erected this cross on the point in their presence and they watched it being put together and set up. And when it had been raised in the air, we all knelt down with our hands joined, worshipping it before them; and made signs to them, looking up and pointing towards heaven, that by means of this we had our redemption, at which they showed many marks of admiration, at the same time turning and looking at the cross.

When we had returned to our ships, the captain [Donnacona, a Huron Indian leader], dressed in an old black bearskin, arrived in a canoe with three of his sons and his brother; but they did not come so close to the ships as they had usually done. And pointing to the cross he made us a long harangue, making the sign of the cross with two of his fingers; and then he pointed to the land all around about, as if he wished to say that all this region belonged to him, and that we ought not to have set up this cross without his permission. And when he had finished his harangue, we held up an axe to him, pretending we would barter it for his skin. To this he nodded assent and little by little drew near the side of our vessel, thinking he would have the axe. But one of our men, who was in our dinghy, caught hold of his canoe, and at once two or three more stepped down into it and made them come on board our vessel, at which they were greatly astonished. When they had come on board, they were assured by the captain that no harm would befall them, while at the same time every sign of affection was shown to them; and they were made to eat and to drink and to be of good cheer. And then we explained to them by signs that the cross had been set up to serve as a landmark

1. Gaspé Harbour, near the mouth of the St. Lawrence River

and guidepost on coming into the harbour, and that we would soon come back and would bring them iron wares and other goods; and that we wished to take two of his sons [named Taignoagny and Dom Agaya] away with us and afterwards would bring them back again to that harbour. And we dressed up his two sons in shirts and ribbons and in red caps, and put a little brass chain round the neck of each, at which they were greatly pleased. [Cartier returned to France and displayed the natives to the royal court. He then voyaged back to North America in 1535 with his two charges. On this trip, he hoped to find the rumored kingdom of Saguenay.]. . .

The Search for Saguenay

On [Friday] the thirteenth of that month [August 1535] we set out from St Lawrence's Bay and heading towards the west, made our way as far as a cape on the south side, which lies some twenty-five leagues west, one quarter southwest of St Lawrence's harbour. And it was told us by the two savages whom we had captured on our first voyage, that this cape formed part of the land on the south which was an island, and that to the south of it lay the route from Honguedo [Gaspé], where we had seized them when on our first voyage, to Canada;[2] and that two days' journey from this cape and island began the kingdom of the Saguenay, on the north shore as one made one's way towards this Canada. . . .

The two savages assured us that this was the way to the mouth of the great river of Hochelaga [the St. Lawrence] and the route towards Canada, and that the river grew narrower as one approached Canada; and also that farther up, the water became fresh, and that one could make one's way so far up the river that they had never heard of anyone reaching the head of it. Furthermore, that one could only proceed along it in small boats. . . .

On [Tuesday], the seventh of the month [September] be-

2. This word is always used to designate the region along the St. Lawrence from Grosse Island on the east to a point between Quebec and Three Rivers on the west.

ing our Lady's day, after hearing mass, we set out from this [Coudres] island to proceed up stream, and came to fourteen islands which lay some seven or eight leagues beyond Coudres Island. This is the point where the province and territory of Canada begins. . . . After we had cast anchor between this large island and the north shore, we went on land and took with us the two men we had seized on our former voyage. We came upon several of the people of the country who began to run away and would not come near, until our two men had spoken to them and told them that they were Taignoagny and Dom Agaya. And when they knew who it was, they began to welcome them, dancing and going through many ceremonies. And some of the headmen came to our longboats, bringing us many eels and other fish, with two or three measures of corn, which is their bread in that country, and many large melons. And during that day many canoes filled with the people of the country, both men as well as women, came to our ships to see and welcome our two men. The Captain received them all well and treated them to what he had to offer. And to ingratiate himself with them, he gave them some small presents of little value, at which they were much pleased.

On the morrow, the lord of Canada, named Donnacona (but as leader they call him *Agouhanna*), came to our ships accompanied by many people in twelve canoes. He then sent back ten of these and came alongside our ships with only two canoes carrying sixteen men. And when he was opposite to the smallest of our three ships [*Emérillon*], this *Agouhanna* began to make a speech and to harangue us, moving his body and his limbs in a marvellous manner, as is their custom when showing joy and contentment. And when he came opposite to the Captain's vessel, on board of which were Taignoagny and Dom Agaya, the leader spoke to them and they to him, telling him what they had seen in France, and the good treatment meted out to them there. At this the leader was much pleased and begged the Captain to stretch out his arms to him that he might hug and kiss them, which is the way they welcome one in that country. . . .

Signs of Distrust

On the following day, we set sail with our ships to bring them to the spot called Ste Croix, where we arrived the next day [Tuesday], the fourteenth of the month. And Donnacona, Taignoagny, and Dom Agaya came to meet us with twenty-five canoes filled with people who were coming from the direction whence we had set out and were making towards Stadacona, which is their home. And all came over towards our ships, showing many signs of joy, except the two men we had brought with us, to wit, Taignoagny and Dom Agaya, who were altogether changed in their attitude and goodwill, and refused to come on board our ships, although many times begged to do so. At this we began somewhat to distrust them. . . .

On the morrow [Thursday], the sixteenth of that month, we placed our two largest vessels inside the harbour and river, where at high water there is a depth of three fathoms, and at low tide, half a fathom. But the bark [smaller ship] was left in the roadstead to take us to Hochelaga [native settlement farther down the St. Lawrence]. And as soon as the two vessels had been brought into the harbour and had grounded, Donnacona, Taignoagny, and Dom Agaya came about them with more than 500 people, both men, women, and children; and the leader came on board with ten or twelve of the headmen of the village, who were feasted and fêted by the Captain and others, according to their rank; and some small presents were given to them. And Taignoagny told the Captain that Donnacona was annoyed because he [Cartier] intended to go to Hochelaga, and was most unwilling that Taignoagny should accompany him, as he had promised to do; for the river was not worth exploring. To this the Captain made reply, that notwithstanding this he would use his efforts to reach there; for he had orders from the king his master to push on as far as possible. . . .

After this Donnacona . . . began a long harangue, holding by the hand a girl of about ten or twelve years of age, whom at length he presented to the Captain. Thereupon the whole of the leader's people raised three shouts and cries in sign of joy and alliance. He next made him a present of two small boys of tenderer age, one after the other, on which the people gave vent to the same shouts and cries as before. After the Captain had thanked the leader for the presents thus made to him, Taignoagny told the Captain that the girl was the daughter of Donnacona's own sister, and that one of the boys was his, the speaker's, brother; and that these children had been given to him to the intent he should not go to Hochelaga. To this our Captain replied that in case they had been given to him with that intent, they must be taken back; for that nothing would induce him to forgo the attempt to make his way to Hochelaga, since such were his orders. On hearing this Dom Agaya, Taignoagny's companion, told the Captain that Donnacona had given him these children out of pure affection and in sign of alliance, and that he [Dom Agaya] was willing to accompany the Captain to Hochelaga. At this Taignoagny and Dom Agaya had high words together, whereby we were convinced, as well from this as by other bad turns we had seen him do, that Taignoagny was a worthless fellow, who was intent on nothing but treason and malice. . . .

The Natives Bring Bad News

On the next day [Saturday], the eighteenth of the month, they devised a great ruse to prevent us still from going to Hochelaga. They dressed up three men as devils, arraying them in black and white dog-skins, with horns as long as one's arm and their faces coloured black as coal, and unknown to us put them into a canoe. They themselves then came towards our ships in a crowd as usual but remained some two hours in the wood without appearing, awaiting the moment when the tide would bring down the above-mentioned canoe. At that hour they all came out of the wood and showed themselves in front of our ships but without coming so near as they were in the habit of doing. . . . Soon after arrived the canoe in which were the three men dressed as devils, with long horns on their heads. And as they drew near, the one in the middle made a wonderful harangue, but they passed by our ships without once turning their faces towards us, and proceeded to head for the shore and to run their canoe on land. Donnacona and his people at once seized the canoe and the three men, who had let themselves fall to the bottom of it like dead men, and carried them, canoe and men, into the wood which was distant a stone's throw from our ships; and not a soul remained in sight but all retired into the wood. And there in the wood they began a preaching and a speechifying that could be heard from our ships, which lasted about half an hour. After that, Taignoagny and Dom Agaya came out of the wood, walking in our direction, with their hands joined and their caps under their arms, pretending to be much astonished. And Taignoagny began to speak and repeated three times, *'Jesus,' 'Jesus,' 'Jesus,'* lifting his eyes towards heaven. Then Dom Agaya called out *'Jesus,' 'Maria,' 'Jacques Cartier,'* looking up to heaven as the other had done. The Captain, seeing their grimaces and gesticulations, began to ask them what was the matter, and what new event had happened? They replied that there was bad news, adding that indeed it was far from good. The Captain again asked them what was the trouble? They answered that their god, Cudouagny by name, had made an announcement at Hochelaga, and that the three above-mentioned men had come in his name to tell them the tidings, which were that there would be so much ice and snow that all would perish. At this we all began to laugh and to tell them that their god Cudouagny was a mere fool who did not know what he was saying; and that they should tell his messengers as much; and that Jesus would keep them safe from the cold if they would trust in him. Thereupon Taignoagny and his companion asked the Captain if he had spoken to Jesus; and he replied that his priests had done so and that there would be fine weather. . . .

Perceptions of Malice

After this, these people used to come day by day to our ships bringing us plenty of eels and other fish to get our wares. We gave them in exchange knives, awls, beads, and other trinkets, which pleased them much. But we perceived that the two rogues whom we had brought with us [Taignoagny and Dom Agaya] were telling them and giving them to understand that what we bartered to them was of no value, and that for what they brought us, they could as easily get hatchets as knives, although the Captain had made them many presents, which indeed they never for a moment ceased begging from him. . . .

Seeing their malice, and fearing lest they should attempt some treasonable design and come against us with a host of people, the Captain gave orders for the fort to be strengthened on every side with large, wide, deep ditches, and with a gate and drawbridge, and with extra logs of wood set crosswise to the former. . . .

Kidnapping Donnacona

The Captain, on being informed of [a] large number of people [gathered] at Stadacona, though unaware of their purpose, yet determined to outwit them and to seize their leader [Donnacona], Taignoagny, Dom Agaya, and the headmen. And moreover he had quite made up his mind to take Donnacona to France, that he might relate and tell to the king all he had seen in the west of the wonders of the world; for he assured us that he had been to the land of the Saguenay where there are immense quantities of gold, rubies, and other rich things, and that the men there are white as in France and go clothed in woollens. He told us also that he had visited another region where the people, possessing no anus, never eat nor digest, but simply make water through the penis. He told us furthermore that he had been in the land of the Picquenyans, and to another country whose inhabitants have only one leg and other marvels too long to relate. This leader is an old man who has never ceased travelling about the country by river, stream, and trail since his earliest recollection. . . .

On [Wednesday] 3 May, which was the festival of the Holy Cross, the Captain in celebration of this solemn feast had a beautiful cross erected some thirty-five feet high. . . . And that day about noon several persons arrived from Stada-

cona, both men, women, and children, who told us that Donnacona with Taignoagny, Dom Agaya, and the rest of their
party were on their way, which pleased us, as we were in
hopes of being able to capture them. . . . As soon as they
came opposite to our ships the Captain went and greeted
Donnacona, who likewise was friendly enough but kept his
eye constantly fixed on the wood and was wonderfully un-
easy. Soon after Taignoagny came up and told Donnacona
that on no account should he go inside the fort. . . . And our
Captain, knowing this, went outside the fort where he had
been keeping and saw that at Taignoagny's warning the
women were hurrying away and that none but men were
left, who were present in considerable numbers. At this the
Captain issued his orders for the seizure of Donnacona,
Taignoagny, Dom Agaya, and two other headmen, whom he
pointed out, and he commanded that the others should be
driven away. Soon after the leader [Donnacona] entered the
fort in company with the Captain, whereupon Taignoagny
immediately rushed in to make him go out again. Seeing
there was no other chance, our Captain proceeded to call to
his men to seize them. At this they rushed forth and laid
hands upon the leader and the others whose capture had
been decided upon. The Canadians, beholding this, began to
flee and to scamper off like sheep before wolves, some
across the river, others into the wood, each seeking his own
safety. When the above-mentioned had been captured and
the rest had all disappeared, Donnacona and his companions
were placed in safe custody.

River of the Amazons

Gaspar de Carvajal

Spanish explorer and soldier Francisco de Orellana arrived in the New World in the 1520s, participating in the conquest of Peru. He subsequently became the first Spanish governor of Guayaquil, Ecuador. He then joined an excursion in 1540 in search of the mythic kingdom of El Dorado. The leader of the expedition was Gonzalo Pizarro, brother of Francisco Pizarro, the conqueror of the Incas.

By 1542, the journey into the heart of South America was not going well and the desperate party faced starvation. Orellana took fifty-seven men to navigate a nearby river in search of food. He and his men were not to rejoin Pizarro, having floated a long way on dangerous rivers upon which they could most likely not safely reverse course. They had little idea of where the waterway would take them, what types of natives they would encounter, or what the geography and climate would hold in store. Seven months later, the group made it to the Atlantic, being the first Europeans to cross the continent on the mighty Amazon. The eyewitness chronicle excerpted below was written by Friar Gaspar de Carvajal, chaplain of Pizarro's expedition.

And so the said Captain Orellana picked out fifty-seven men, with whom he embarked in the aforesaid boat and in certain canoes which they had taken away from the Indians, and he began to proceed down his river with the idea of promptly turning back if food was found; all of which turned out just the reverse of what we all expected, because we did not find food for a distance of two hundred

Gaspar de Carvajal, "Discovery of the Orellana River," *The Discovery of the Amazon*, edited by H.C. Heaton and translated by Bertram T. Lee. New York: American Geographical Society, 1934.

leagues, nor were we finding any [for ourselves], from which cause we suffered very great privation. . . .

Starvation

On the second day after we had set out and separated from our companions we were almost wrecked in the middle of the river because the boat struck a log and it [i.e., the log] stove in one of its planks, so that if we had not been close to land we should have ended our journey there; but matters were soon remedied [thanks to the energy of the men] in hauling the boat out of water and fastening a piece of plank on it, and we promptly started off on our way with very great haste; and, as the river flowed fast, we proceeded on at the rate of from twenty to twenty-five leagues [a day], for now the river was high and [its power] increased owing to the effect of many other rivers which emptied into it on the right from a southerly direction. We journeyed on for three days without [finding] any inhabited country at all. Seeing that we had come far away from where our companions had stopped and that we had used up what little food we had brought along, [too little] for so uncertain a journey as the one that we were pursuing, the Captain and the companions conferred about the difficulty [we were in], and the [question of] turning back, and the lack of food. . . . And so, after taking counsel as to what should be done, talking over our affliction and hardships, it was decided that we should choose of two evils the one which to the Captain and to all should appear to be the lesser, which was to go forward and follow the river, [and thus] either die or see what there was along it, trusting in Our Lord that He would see fit to preserve our lives until we should see our way out; and in the meantime, lacking other victuals, we reached a [state of] privation so great that we were eating nothing but leather, belts and soles of shoes, cooked with certain herbs, with the result that so great was our weakness that we could not remain standing. . . .

Extraordinary Dangers

And so we began to move on, . . . and we had not gone a distance of something like twenty leagues, when there joined with our river another one from the right, not very wide, on which river an important overlord named Irrimorrany had his abode, and, because he was an Indian and overlord of much intelligence and because he had come to see the Captain and bring him food, he [i.e., the Captain] wanted to go to his country; but [in addition to other difficulties in the way of doing so] there was also the reason that the river came down very strong and with a great onrush; and here we were on the point of perishing, because, right there where this river flowed into the one on which we were navigating, the one stream battled with the other and [the waters thus stirred up] sent large pieces of driftwood from one side to the other, so that it was hard work to navigate up it, because it [i.e., the river] formed many whirlpools and carried us from one bank to the other; but by dint of hard work we got out of this danger, [though] without being able to reach the village, and we passed on toward where we had heard that there was another village which they told us was two hundred leagues farther on from there, all the country between being barren, and so we covered them [i.e., the two hundred leagues] at the cost of a great deal of suffering for our bodies, passing through many hardships and very extraordinary dangers, for example when there befell us a certain mishap and [one which caused us] no small worry for the time that we were held up by it, and this was that two canoes carrying eleven Spaniards of ours became lost among some islands without knowing where we were and without our being able to find them; they were lost for two days without being able to locate us, and we, expecting never to see them again, for the time being experienced very great grief; but at the end of the aforesaid time Our Lord was pleased that we should come together, so that there was no little rejoicing among [us] all. . . .

Endless Running Battles

The brigantes [boats] being ready and unmoored and the oars in hand, the Captain with the companions in good order went down [to the river], and they embarked, and he put off, and was not a stone's throw away when there came more than four hundred Indians on the water and along the land, and, as those on the land could not get at us, they served no purpose but to call and shout; and those on the water attacked again and again, like men who had been wronged, with great fury; but our companions with their crossbows [and] arquebuses [early type of rifle] defended the brigantines so well that they turned away those wicked people. This was around sundown, and in this manner, attacking us every little while, [they kept] following us all the night, for not one moment did they allow us a respite, because they had us headed off. In this way we kept on until it was day, when we saw ourselves in the midst of numerous and very large settlements, whence fresh Indians were constantly coming out, while those who were fatigued dropped out. About midday, when our companions were no longer able to row, we were all thoroughly exhausted from the cruel night and from the fighting which the Indians had forced upon us. The Captain, in order that the men might get a little rest and eat something, gave orders that we put in on an uninhabited island which was in the middle of the river, and, just as they began to cook something to eat, there came along a great number of canoes, and they attacked us three times, so that they put us in great distress. It having become evident to the Indians that from the water they could not put us to rout, they decided to attack us [both] by land and by water, because, as there were many Indians, there were enough of them for [undertaking] anything. The Captain, seeing what the Indians were making ready to do, decided not to wait for them on land, and hence embarked again and pulled out into the river, because there he thought he could better fight back, and thus we began to move on, with the Indians still not ceasing to follow us and force upon us many combats, because from these settlements there had gathered together many Indians and on the land the men who appeared were beyond count. . . .

A Village

We had gone, from the time we left [the province of] Aparia . . . three hundred and forty leagues, of which two hundred

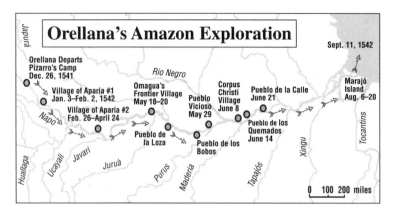

were [country] without any settlements. . . .

We saw emptying into the river another very powerful and wider river on the right . . . and at this junction of the two [rivers] there were numerous and very large settlements and very pretty country and very fruitful land: all this, now, lay in the dominion and land of Omagua, and, because the villages were so numerous and so large and because there were so many inhabitants, the Captain did not wish to make port, and so all that day we passed through settled country with occasional fighting, because on the water they attacked us so pitilessly that they made us go down mid-river; and many times the Indians started to converse with us, and, as we did not understand them, we did not know what they were saying to us. At the hour of vespers we came to a village that was on a high bank, and as it appeared small to us the Captain ordered us to capture it . . . and the Indians put up a defense for more than an hour, but in the end they were beaten and we were masters of the village, where we found very great quantities of food, of which we laid in a supply. In this village there was a villa in which there was a great deal of porcelain ware of various makes, both jars and pitchers, very large . . . and other small pieces such as plates and bowls and candelabra of this porcelain of the best that has ever been seen in the world . . . because it . . . is all glazed and embellished with all colors, and so bright [are these colors] that they astonish, and, more than this, the drawings and paintings which they make on them are so accurately worked out that [one wonders how] with [only] natural skill they manufacture and decorate all these things [making them look just] like Roman [articles]; and here the Indians told us that as much as there was made out of clay in this house, so much there was back in the country in gold and silver, and [they said] that they would take us there, for it was near. . . . And in this village also there were gold and silver; but, as our intention was merely to search for something to eat and see to it that we saved our lives and gave an account of such a great accomplishment, we did not concern ourselves with, nor were we interested in, any wealth. . . .

Dominion of the Amazons

On the following Thursday we passed by other villages of medium size, and we made no attempt to stop there. . . . God willed that, on rounding a bend which the river made, we should see on the shore ahead many villages, and very large ones, which shone white. Here we came suddenly upon the excellent land and dominion of the Amazons. These said villages had been forewarned and knew of our coming, in consequence whereof they [i.e., the inhabitants] came out on the water to meet us, in no friendly mood, and, when they had come close to the Captain, he would have liked to induce them to accept peace, and so he began to speak to them and call them, but they laughed, and mocked us and came up close to us and told us to keep on going and [added] that down below they were waiting for us, and that there they were to seize us all and take us to the Amazons. The Captain, angered at the arrogance of the Indians, gave orders to shoot at them with the crossbows and arquebuses, so that they might reflect and become aware that we had wherewith to assail them. . . . In view of the danger that we were in, the Captain began to cheer up the men at the oars and urge them to make haste to beach the brigantines, and so, although with hard work, we succeeded in beaching the boats and our companions jumped into the water, which came up to their chests: here there was fought a very serious and hazardous battle, because the Indians were there mixed in among our Spaniards, who defended them-

selves so courageously that it was a marvelous thing to behold.
More than an hour was taken up by this fight, for the Indians
did not lose spirit, rather it seemed as if it was being doubled
in them, although they saw many of their own number killed,
and they passed over them [i.e., their bodies], and they merely
kept retreating and coming back again. I want it to be known
what the reason was why these Indians defended themselves
in this manner. It must be explained that they are the subjects
of, and tributaries to, the Amazons, and, our coming having
been made known to them, they went to them to ask help, and
there came as many as ten or twelve of them, for we ourselves
saw these women, who were there fighting in front of all the
Indian men as women captains, and these latter fought so
courageously that the Indian men did not dare to turn their
backs, and anyone who did turn his back they killed with clubs
right there before us, and this is the reason why the Indians
kept up their defense for so long. These women are very white
and tall, and have hair very long and braided and wound about
the head, and they are very robust and go about naked, [but]
with their privy parts covered, with their bows and arrows in
their hands, doing as much fighting as ten Indian men, and indeed there was one woman among these who shot an arrow a
span deep into one of the brigantines, and others less deep, so
that our brigantines looked like porcupines. . . .

Because there were many warriors coming from the other
villages to give aid and as they were bound to turn back [on
us], since already they were again giving their calls, the
Captain ordered the men to get into the boats with very great
haste, for he did not wish to jeopardize the lives of all, and
so they got into the boats, not without some trouble, because
already the Indians were beginning to fight [again], and besides this there was approaching on the water a great fleet
of canoes, and so we pushed out into the river and got away
from the shore. . . .

Amazon Civilization

That night we managed to get to a place to sleep, now outside of this whole settled region. . . .

In this stopping-place the Captain took [aside an] Indian who had been captured farther back, because he now understood him by means of a list of words that he had made. . . . The Captain asked him what women those were [who] had come to help them and fight against us; the Indian said that they were certain women who resided in the interior of the country, a seven day journey from the shore. . . . The Captain asked him if these women were married: the Indian said they were not. The Captain asked him about how they lived: the Indian replied [first] that, as he had already said, they were off in the interior of the land and that he had been there many times and had seen their customs and mode of living, for as their vassal he was in the habit of going there to carry the tribute whenever the overlord sent him. The Captain asked if these women were numerous: the Indian said that they were, and that he knew by name seventy villages. . . . The Captain asked if these women bore children: the Indian answered that they did. The Captain asked him how, not being married and there being no man residing among them, they became pregnant: he said that these Indian women consorted with Indian men at times, and, when that desire came to them, they assembled a great horde of warriors and went off to make war on a very great overlord whose residence is not far from that [i.e. the land] of these women, and by force they brought them to their own country and kept them with them for the time that suited their caprice, and after they found themselves pregnant they sent them back to their country without doing them any harm; and afterwards, when the time came for them to have children, if they gave birth to male children, they killed them and sent them to their fathers, and, if female children, they raised them with great solemnity and instructed them in the arts of war. He said furthermore that among all these women there was one ruling mistress who subjected and held under her hand and jurisdiction all the rest, which mistress went by the name of Coñori. He said that there was [in their possession] a very great wealth of gold and silver and that [in the case of] all the mistresses of rank and distinction their eating utensils were nothing but gold or silver. . . . He said in addition that in this land, as we understood him, there were camels that carried them [i.e., the inhabitants] on their backs, and he said that there were other animals, which we did not succeed in understanding about, which were as big as horses and which had hair as long as the spread of the thumb and forefinger, measured from tip to tip, and cloven hoofs, and that people kept them tied up. . . . He related that they had a rule to the effect that when the sun went down no male Indian was to remain [anywhere] in all of these cities, but that any such must depart and go to his country; he said in addition that many Indian provinces bordering on them were held in subjection by them and made to pay tribute and to serve them. . . .

The next day, in the morning, we departed from this stopping-place in the oak grove, not a little delighted, thinking that we were leaving all the settled country behind us and that we were going to have an opportunity to rest from our hardships.

Chapter 5

Seventeenth-Century Expansion

Chapter Preface

D uring the sixteenth and seventeenth centuries, many of the same attractions that drew Europeans to the New World motivated France, Spain, and England in their explorations of North America. Though the myths of fantastically wealthy kingdoms were fading, and the dream of an easy water passage to Asia seemed increasingly doubtful, the goals of conversion and of extending each country's influence across the sea remained. In fact, an important concern for each country was the presence and continued expansion of the other two in the New World.

By the late 1500s, Spain and England especially viewed each other warily in North America. The Spanish established military outposts and missions in the 1560s in and around the coast of Florida. In 1588 naval fleets of the two rivals met in the English Channel, with the English winning a decisive victory over the Spanish Armada. The English then intensified their attention to North America, establishing colonies in Roanoke in 1587, Jamestown and Sagadahoc in 1607, and Plymouth in 1620.

Far from the east coast, the Spanish also established a colony in the province of New Mexico by 1600, following up on earlier inroads in the southwest made by missionaries. At roughly the same time, the French were establishing fur-trading outposts along the St. Lawrence River and working their way inland. The French also strengthened their presence through forging commercial and military alliances with native peoples. French settlements farther south had not fared so well; a 1564 settlement of French Huguenots (Calvinists) near present-day Jacksonville, Florida, was razed by the Spanish the next year, killing all male settlers.

By the time of French Jesuit missionary Jacques Marquette's 1673 expedition from upper Lake Michigan across

Wisconsin and down the Mississippi, settlers from each of these three countries were still very conscious of each other's presence. In fact, one reason Marquette's journal gives for his party's reluctance to follow the Mississippi all the way to the Gulf of Mexico was the presence of Spaniards who might intercept them.

The competing presence of each country lasted well beyond this period. It was with the French that Thomas Jefferson negotiated the Louisiana Purchase in 1803, through which the young American nation recently separated from England acquired a huge and uncharted territory from the Mississippi to the Rocky Mountains. Spain controlled Florida until 1819, and the United States added the former Spanish territories in the southwest and west through its invasion of Mexico in 1846.

Exploring the Spanish Southwest

Juan de Oñate

In the late fifteenth century, interest was rekindled in areas of what would later become the southwestern United States. The Spanish province of New Mexico was largely unexplored territory, and was even thought to extend to what is now Canada. In addition to the goal of converting the natives, Spanish authorities also held out hope that New Mexico might contain great natural resources and wealth like Cortés's Mexico, and that the new territory might still yield a strait that would open a sea route to Asia.

Juan de Oñate was from a wealthy and aristocratic Spanish family; his father held a prestigious position in Mexico and Juan was born there. As a young man, Oñate had led campaigns to pacify Indians near the northern outposts of Mexico, and in 1595 he was awarded the highly prized contract to colonize and explore well beyond the last outpost in Mexico. He set out in 1598 with approximately five hundred people, including soldiers and their families, Mexican Indians, and African slaves, and pushed northward more than six hundred miles to extend Spanish influence into what is now northern New Mexico.

A few years later, he ventured east and then north again. It is from Oñate's account of this second expedition that the following extracts are taken. In it, he describes his relations with native tribes who had already had some interaction with Europeans, his reactions to the wondrous "monstrous cattle" encountered along the way, and the long march to the region

Herbert Eugene Bolton, ed., *Spanish Exploration in the Southwest, 1542–1706*. New York: Barnes & Noble, 1963.

known as "Quivira," near present-day Wichita, Kansas. Oñate's demands of obedience to the crown and subduing and massacre of native pueblos and villages have led some to call him "the last conquistador."

With particular care . . . and after many supplications, suffrages, sacrifices, and prayers to God our Lord, that his Majesty might reveal His divine will, knowing that that of our most Catholic king and lord Philip, God guard him through infinite years, has been and is that the most holy name of God be proclaimed in these his realms, and His holy gospel preached to these barbarous nations, bound by the power of Satan, the enemy of humankind, the governor and adelantado Don Juan de Oñate determined to make an expedition from these first settlements[1] where at the present time this camp of his Majesty is established, to the interior, by a northern route and direction, both because of the splendid reports which the native Indians were giving of this land, and also because of what an Indian named Joseph, who was born and reared in New Spain [Mexico] and who speaks the Mexican tongue, saw while going with Captain Umaña.[2]

The most necessary things having been arranged for the journey, with the supply of provisions, arms, ammunition, and other requisite military stores, with more than seventy picked men for the expedition, all very well equipped, more than seven hundred horses and mules, six mule carts, and two carts drawn by oxen conveying four pieces of artillery, and with servants to carry the necessary baggage, the journey was begun this year of 1601, the said adelantado, Don Juan de Oñate, governor and captain-general, going as commander, with Vicente de Çaldivar Mendoça as his *maese de campo* and *sargento mayor*, and two religious of the order of our father San Francisco, Fray Francisco de Velasco, priest, and Fray Pedro de Vergara, lay brother. . . .

1. At San Juan, near modern-day Santa Fe, New Mexico. Oñate established these settlements on his 1598 expedition.   2. Antonio Gutiérrez de Humaña was killed by Indians during an unauthorized 1593 expedition that took him on a route similar to Oñate's journey.

Plains of the Apache

At times it became necessary for us to depart from the main river in order to find a road for the carts; and although we feared the lack of watering places for the cattle, there are so many in this country that throughout the journey at distances of three or four leagues there was always sufficient water for the cattle and for the men; and in many places there were springs of very good water and groves of trees.

In some places we came across camps of people of the Apache nation, who are the ones who possess these plains [in the vicinity of the modern-day Texas panhandle], and who, having neither fixed place nor site of their own, go from place to place with the cattle always following them. We were not disturbed by them at all, although we were in their land, nor did any Indian become impertinent. We therefore passed on, always close to the river, and although on one day we might be delayed in our journey by a very heavy rain, such as are very common in those plains, on the following day and thereafter we journeyed on, sometimes crossing the river at very good fords.

Each day the land through which we were travelling became better, and the luxury of an abundance of fish from the river greatly alleviated the hardships of the journey. And the fruits gave no less pleasure, particularly the plums, of a hundred thousand different kinds, as mellow and good as those which grow in the choicest orchards of our land. They are so good that although eaten by thousands they never injured anybody. The trees were small, but their fruit was more plentiful than their leaves. . . .

Monstrous Cattle

Proceeding on the day of the Glorious Levite and Martyr, San Lorenzo, God was pleased that we should begin to see those most monstrous cattle called *cibola* [buffalo]. Although they were very fleet of foot, on this day four or five of the bulls were killed, which caused great rejoicing. On the following day, continuing our journey, we now saw great droves of bulls and cows, and from there on the multitude which we saw was so great that it might be considered a falsehood by one who had not seen them, for, according to the judgment of all of us who were in any army, nearly every day and wherever we went as many cattle came out as are to be found in the largest ranches of New Spain, and they were so tame that nearly always, unless they were chased or frightened, they remained quiet and did not flee. The flesh of these cattle is very good, and very much better than that of our cows. In general they are very fat, especially the cows, and almost all have a great deal of tallow. By experience we noted that they do not become angry like our cattle, and are never dangerous.

All these cattle are of one color, namely brown, and it was a great marvel to see a white bull in such a multitude. Their form is so frightful that one can only infer that they are a mixture of different animals. The bulls and the cows alike are humped, the curvature extending the whole length of the back and even over the shoulders. And although the entire body is covered with wool, on the hump, from the middle of the body to the head, the breast, and the forelegs, to just above the knee, the wool is much thicker, and so fine and soft that it could be spun and woven like that of the Castilian sheep. It is a very savage animal, and is incomparably larger than our cattle, although it looks small because of its short legs. Its hide is of the thickness of that of our cattle, and the native Indians are so expert in dressing the hides that they convert them into clothing. . . .

Camp of the Escanjaques

From this point the *maese de campo* began again to explore the country, and having travelled three leagues he discovered a large ranchería, with more than five thousand souls; and although the people were warlike, as it later developed, and although at first they began to place themselves in readiness to fight, by signs of peace they were given to understand that we were not warriors, and they became so friendly with us that some of them came that night to our camp and entertained us with wonderful reports of the people further on. . . .

At three in the afternoon we arrived within an arquebus [early gun] shot of this ranchería, and at some pools that were there we stopped with due care and precaution. From there the governor and the religious went with more than thirty armed horsemen to reconnoitre the people and the ranchería, and they, all drawn up in regular order in front of their ranchos, began to raise the palms of their hands towards the sun, which is the sign of peace among them. Assuring them that peace was what we wanted, all the people, women, youths, and small children, came to where we were; and they consented to our visiting their houses, which all consisted of branches an *estado* and a half long, placed in a circle, some of them being so wide that they were ninety feet in diameter. Most of them were covered with tanned hides, which made them resemble tents. They were not a people who sowed or reaped, but they lived solely on the cattle. They were ruled and governed by chiefs, and like communities which are freed from subjection to any lord, they obeyed their chiefs but little. . . .

Nations in Conflict

We learned while here that this nation was at war with the people settled eight leagues distant towards the interior, and they, thinking that we were going to avenge the murder of the Spaniards who had entered with Umaña, of course took the opportunity to throw the blame upon their enemies and to tell us that it was they who had killed them. Thinking that we were going for this purpose only, they were much pleased, and offered to accompany us, and as we were unable to prevent it, lest we should cause them to make trouble, they went. . . .

We set out . . . the next day, and, leaving the river and passing through some pleasant plains, after having travelled four leagues we began to see people who appeared upon some elevations of a hill. Although hostile to this nation they came on, inviting us to battle and war, shouting and throwing dirt into the air, which is the sign used in all this region to proclaim cruel war. Three or four hundred people awaited us in peace, and by the signs which one side was able to make to the other we were assured of friendship. Peace being made, some of these people came to us, and throwing among us some beads which they wore about their necks, proclaimed themselves our friends. . . .

Signs of Previous Expeditions

All that night we took the necessary care and precaution, but at dawn the following day the people who had represented themselves as friendly to us were stationed at our rear in a great multitude, threatening the other tribe "to beat a Roldan," and awaiting their chance to attack them. We inquiring again regarding the country, they told us that in this region they had murdered the Spaniards [the Humaña party] surrounding them with fire and burning them all, and that they had with them one who had escaped, injured by the fire. Counsel and opinion being taken as to what must be done in a matter of such importance, it was decided to seize some Indians, both to take with us as guides and also to verify the statements of their enemies, and it was a fortunate coincidence that their chief, or captain, whom they call Catarax, was there at the time. It was remarkable to note how they obeyed him and served him, like a people more united, peaceful, and settled. As evidence of this it is enough to say that while they might with justice have become aroused because of his arrest, they did not do so, merely because he signalled to them that they should withdraw.

The Rich Settlements of Quivira

We took him with us, treating him well, as was proper, and in order to carry out our plans we crossed the river, at a very good ford. Having travelled half a league we came to a settlement containing more than twelve hundred houses, all established along the bank of another good-sized river which flowed into the large one [the Arkansas in south central Kansas]. They were all round, built of forked poles and bound with rods, and on the outside covered to the ground with dry grass. Within, on the sides, they had frameworks or platforms which served them as beds on which they slept. Most of them were large enough to hold eight or ten persons. . . . They ascended to this platform by means of a movable wooden ladder. Not a house lacked these platforms. We found the pueblo entirely deserted but not lacking maize, of which there was much and of good quality. For this reason the enemy wished to sack it; but in no manner were they permitted to do so, nor to do any damage except to take away a little maize. Thereupon the governor dismissed them and gave them express commands to go to their ranchería, which they did.

We remained here for one day in this pleasant spot surrounded on all sides by fields of maize and crops of the Indians. The stalks of the maize were as high as that of New Spain and in many places even higher. The land was so rich that, having harvested the maize, a new growth of a span in height had sprung up over a large portion of the same ground, without any cultivation or labor other than the removal of the weeds and the making of holes where they planted the maize. There were many beans, some gourds, and, between the fields, some plum trees. The crops were not irrigated but dependent on the rains, which, as we noted, must be very regular in that land, because in the month of October it rained as it does in August in New Spain. It was thought certain that it had a warm climate, for the people we saw went about naked, although they wore skins. Like the other settled Indians they utilize cattle in large numbers. It is incredible how many there are in that land.

Turning Back

Here we took new information from the Indian, who appeared to be one of the *caciques* or lords of the land, regarding what there was further ahead, and he informed us that up the river were settled people like these in large numbers, and that at one side was another large river which divided into six or seven branches, on all of which there were many people, and that the people whom Umaña had brought had been killed eighteen days' journey from here. . . . They accordingly persuaded us that under no circumstances should we proceed, saying that the people who had withdrawn from this settlement had done so in order on the third day to assemble their friends, who were so numerous that in the course of a whole day they would not be able to pass by their houses, and that undoubtedly, our number being so small, they would soon put an end to us, not a single person escaping.

Although this spurred us on to go ahead, on the following day, having travelled three leagues, all the way through a populated district, and seeing that the houses continued beyond, and having positive knowledge of the large assemblage of people which was awaiting us, it was necessary to take counsel as to what should be done. And seeing that the horses and mules were tired out and exhausted, because of the many leagues travelled, and that the chief purpose of our journey had been achieved, and that his Majesty would be better served by learning the wonders of this land, that he might issue the orders most necessary to the royal service and to the acceleration of the salvation of these souls, and seeing that it would be foolhardy for our small number to proceed where more than three hundred persons were necessary, it was unanimously agreed to present a petition to the governor and adelantado, representing to him the combination of just reasons for not proceeding, making known to him how much greater service would be rendered to his Majesty by informing him of the fertility of the soil, of its many people, of the wealth of the innumerable cattle, so beyond number that they alone would suffice to enrich thousands of men with suet, tallow, and hides; of the suitableness of the land for founding many important settlements, fortunately possessing all materials necessary for the purpose; and above all, of how important it was that the King our Lord should speedily learn what all the world had so much desired to know, so that his Majesty's orders might be carried out; and although it was a hard blow to the governor's courage and bravery, and though he was very sorry to curtail his journey, upon realizing the justness of the petition made in his Majesty's name, he granted it.

Making Native Allies and Enemies

Samuel de Champlain

Samuel de Champlain was a Frenchman who first came to the New World as a ship captain in the service of Spain in 1599. Returning a few years later to France, he published an account of his trip and of the natural riches and government practices in the Spanish colonies. By 1603 he had been assigned to a French expedition following up on the Jacques Cartier expeditions of the 1530s to the St. Lawrence gulf region in Canada, with the goals of converting natives, expanding the fur trade, and searching for riches and the elusive passage across the continent.

In his years in North America, Champlain established settlements, such as the first one at the city of Quebec, and made extensive maps of the region based on his many explorations, which took him along the eastern coast from Maine as far south as current-day Cape Cod. His interest in establishing settlements that relied on the commerce of the fur trade also led to the formation of alliances with several Indian nations including the Algonquins, the Hurons, and the Montagnais. He fought with these natives against their common enemy, the Iroquois, who were primarily based in and around the region that is now part of upstate New York.

The following extracts from Champlain's writings describe a 1609 expedition with his Indian allies against the Iroquois. In it, Champlain also reports the military customs of his native friends that included their practices of listening to soothsayers and interpreting dreams before battle. The mili-

Samuel de Champlain, *Voyages of Samuel de Champlain, 1604–1618*, edited by W.L. Grant. New York: Charles Scribner's Sons, 1907.

tary foray itself led the Frenchman to find a large inland lake—now called Lake Champlain—in the border region between what is now Quebec, New York, and Vermont.

I set out accordingly from the fall of the Iroquois River on the [12th] of July. All the savages set to carrying their canoes, arms, and baggage overland, some half a league, in order to pass by the violence and strength of the fall, which was speedily accomplished. . . . The savages made a review of all their followers, finding that there were twenty-four canoes, with sixty men. After the review was completed, we continued our course to an island, three leagues long, filled with the finest pines I had ever seen. Here they went hunting, and captured some wild animals. Proceeding about three leagues farther on, we made a halt, in order to rest the coming night.

They all at once set to work, some to cut wood, and others to obtain the bark of trees for covering their cabins, for the sake of sheltering themselves, others to fell large trees for constructing a barricade on the river-bank around their cabins, which they do so quickly that in less than two hours so much is accomplished that five hundred of their enemies would find it very difficult to dislodge them without killing large numbers. They make no barricade on the river-bank, where their canoes are drawn up, in order that they may be able to embark, if occasion requires. . . .

Rogue Soothsayers

In all their encampments, they have their Pilotois, or Ostemoy, a class of persons who play the part of soothsayers, in whom these people have faith. One of these builds a cabin, surrounds it with small pieces of wood, and covers it with his robe: after it is built, he places himself inside, so as not to be seen at all, when he seizes and shakes one of the posts of his cabin, muttering some words between his teeth, by which he says he invokes the devil, who appears to him in the form of a stone, and tells him whether they will meet their enemies and kill many of them. This Pilotois lies prostrate on the ground, motionless, only speaking with the devil: on a sudden, he rises to his feet, talking, and tormenting himself in such a manner that, although naked, he is all of a perspiration. All the people surround the cabin, seated on their buttocks, like apes. They frequently told me that the shaking of the cabin, which I saw, proceeded from the devil, who made it move, and not the man inside, although I could see the contrary; for, as I have stated above, it was the Pilotois who took one of the supports of the cabin, and made it move in this manner. They told me also that I should see fire come out from the top, which I did not see at all. These rogues counterfeit also their voice, so that it is heavy and clear, and speak in a language unknown to the other savages. And, when they represent it as broken, the savages think that the devil is speaking, and telling them what is to happen in their war, and what they must do.

Samuel de Champlain

But all these scapegraces, who play the soothsayer, out of a hundred words do not speak two that are true, and impose upon these poor people. There are enough like them in the world, who take food from the mouths of the people by their impostures, as these worthies do. I often remonstrated with the people, telling them that all they did was sheer nonsense, and that they ought not to put confidence in them.

A Disciplined Army

Now, after ascertaining from their soothsayers what is to be their fortune, the chiefs take sticks a foot long, and as many as there are soldiers. They take others, somewhat larger, to indicate the chiefs. Then they go into the wood, and seek out a level place, five or six feet square, where the chief, as sergeant-major, puts all the sticks in such order as seems to him best. Then he calls all his companions, who come all armed; and he indicates to them the rank and order they are to observe in battle with their enemies. All the savages watch carefully this proceeding, observing attentively the outline which their chief has made with the sticks. Then they go away, and set to placing themselves in such order as the sticks were in, when they mingle with each other, and return again to their proper order, which manœuvre they repeat two or three times, and at all their encampments, without needing a sergeant to keep them in the proper order, which they are able to keep accurately without any confusion. This is their rule in war.

We set out on the next day, continuing our course in the river as far as the entrance of the lake. There are many pretty islands here, low, and containing very fine woods and meadows, with abundance of fowl and such animals of the chase as stags, fallow-deer, fawns, roe-bucks, bears, and others, which go from the main land to these islands. We captured a large number of these animals. There are also many beavers, not only in this river, but also in numerous other little ones that flow into it. These regions, although they are pleasant, are not inhabited by any savages, on account of their wars; but they withdraw as far as possible from the rivers into the interior, in order not to be suddenly surprised.

The next day we entered the lake [Lake Champlain] which is of great extent, say eighty or a hundred leagues long, where I saw four fine islands, ten, twelve, and fifteen leagues long, which were formerly inhabited by the savages, like the River of the Iroquois; but they have been abandoned since the wars of the savages with one another prevail. . . .

Champlain's Dream

Now, as we began to approach within two or three days' journey of the abode of their enemies, we advanced only at night, resting during the day. But they did not fail to practise constantly their accustomed superstitions, in order to ascertain what was to be the result of their undertaking; and they often asked me if I had had a dream, and seen their enemies, to which I replied in the negative. Yet I did not cease to encourage them, and inspire in them hope. When night came, we set out on the journey until the next day, when we withdrew into the interior of the forest, and spent the rest of the day there. About ten or eleven o'clock, after taking a little walk about our encampment, I retired. While sleeping, I dreamed that I saw our enemies, the Iroquois, drowning in the lake near a mountain, within sight. When I expressed a wish to help them, our allies, the savages, told me we must let them all die, and that they were of no importance. When I awoke, they did not fail to ask me, as usual, if I had had a dream. I told them that I had, in fact, had a dream. This, upon being related, gave them so much confidence that they did not doubt any longer that good was to happen to them.

The Battle Begins

When it was evening, we embarked in our canoes to continue our course; and, as we advanced very quietly and without making any noise, we met on the 29th of the month the Iroquois, about ten o'clock at evening, at the extremity of a cape which extends into the lake on the western bank. They had come to fight. . . .

Our forces also passed the entire night, their canoes being drawn up close to each other, and fastened to poles, so that they might not get separated, and that they might be all in readiness to fight, if occasion required. We were out upon the water, within arrow range of their barricades. When they were armed and in array, they despatched two canoes by themselves to the enemy to inquire if they wished to fight, to which the latter replied that they wanted nothing else: but they said that, at present, there was not much light, and that it would be necessary to wait for daylight, so as to be able to recognize each other; and that, as soon as the sun rose, they would offer us battle. This was agreed to by our side. Meanwhile, the entire night was spent in dancing and singing, on both sides, with endless insults and other talk; as, how little courage we had, how feeble a resistance we should make against their arms, and that, when day came, we should realize it to our ruin. Ours also were not slow in retorting, telling them they would see such execution of arms as never before, together with an abundance of such talk as is not unusual in the siege of a town. . . .

As soon as we had landed, they [our allies] began to run for some two hundred paces towards their enemies, who stood firmly, not having as yet noticed my companions, who went into the woods with some savages. Our men began to call me with loud cries; and, in order to give me a passage-way, they opened in two parts, and put me at their head, where I marched some twenty paces in advance of the rest, until I was within about thirty paces of the enemy, who at once noticed me, and, halting, gazed at me, as I did also at them. When I saw them making a move to fire at us, I rested my musket against my cheek, and aimed directly at one of the three chiefs. With the same shot, two fell to the ground; and one of their men was so wounded that he died some time after. I had loaded my musket with four balls. When our side saw this shot so favorable for them, they began to raise such loud cries that one could not have heard it thunder. Meanwhile, the arrows flew on both sides. The Iroquois were greatly astonished that two men had been so quickly killed, although they were equipped with armor woven from cotton thread, and with wood which was proof against their arrows. This caused great alarm among them. As I was loading again, one of my companions fired a shot from the woods, which astonished them anew to such a degree that, seeing their chiefs dead, they lost courage, and took to flight, abandoning their camp and fort, and fleeing into the woods whither I pursued them, killing still more of them.

Navigating the "Great River of the West"

Jacques Marquette

In competition with the English and the Spanish in North America, the French in the mid to late seventeenth century began expanding south from their colonies in Canada. Spreading a fur-trading empire into the Great Lakes region— an endeavor facilitated by alliances with many Indian tribes— the French then sent fur trader Louis Jolliet and Jesuit missionary Jacques Marquette on a mission to the Mississippi River. This territory was largely unexplored, and these two are widely credited as being the first Europeans to navigate this vital waterway.

Father Jacques Marquette, who has been credited with authorship of the journal from which the following extracts are taken, had been sent to the Canadian mission of the Jesuits in 1666. He learned many native languages and spent the next several years reaching out to Algonquin Indians in what is present-day northern Michigan, between lakes Michigan, Superior, and Huron.

In 1673, Marquette and Jolliet and five other Frenchmen— often accompanied and piloted by Indian guides—canoed through the northern part of Lake Michigan to Green Bay, and traveled across Wisconsin on foot and via rivers until arriving at the Mississippi. While Marquette stresses his duty and devotion to the mission of conversion, the French clearly were not only compelled to find out where the Mississippi ended, but also to search for a river passage across the continent to the "Southern Sea"—the Pacific Ocean.

Jacques Marquette, *Voyages of Marquette*. Ann Arbor, MI: University Microfilms, 1966.

With all these precautions, we joyfully plied our paddles on a portion of Lake Huron, on that of the Ilinois [Lake Michigan] and on the Bay des Puants [Green Bay].

The first nation that we came to was that of the Folle Avoine [Menominee Indians, on the western shore of Green Bay]. I entered their river, to go and visit these peoples to whom we have preached the Gospel for several years,—in consequence of which, there are several good christians among them. . . .

A Warning

I told these peoples of the Folle Avoine of my design to go and discover those remote nations, in order to teach them the mysteries of our holy religion. They were greatly surprised to hear it, and did their best to dissuade me. They represented to me that I would meet nations who never show mercy to strangers, but break their heads without any cause; and that war was kindled between various peoples who dwelt upon our route, which exposed us to the further manifest danger of being killed by the bands of warriors who are ever in the field. They also said that the great river was very dangerous, when one does not know the difficult places; that it was full of horrible monsters, which devoured men and canoes together; that there was even a demon, who was heard from a great distance, who barred the way, and swallowed up all who ventured to approach him; finally that the heat was so excessive in those countries that it would inevitably cause our death. . . .

Arrival at the Great River of the West

[After crossing Wisconsin via the difficult Fox and Wisconsin rivers,] we safely entered Mississippi of the 17th of June, with a joy that I cannot express.

Here we are, then, on this so renowned river, all of whose peculiar features I have endeavored to note carefully. The Missisipi River takes its rise in various lakes in the country of the northern nations. It is narrow at the place where Miskous [Wisconsin River] empties; its current, which flows southward, is slow and gentle. To the right is a large chain of very high mountains, and to the left are beautiful lands; in various places, the stream is divided by islands. On sounding, we found ten brasses [fathoms] of water. Its width is very unequal; sometimes it is three-quarters of a league, and sometimes it narrows to three arpents [approximately the width of an acre]. We gently followed its course, which runs toward the south and southeast, as far as the 42nd degree of latitude. Here we plainly saw that its aspect was completely changed. There are hardly any woods or mountains; the islands are more beautiful, and are covered with finer trees. We saw only deer and cattle, bustards, and swans without wings, because they drop their plumage in this country. From time to time, we came upon monstrous fish, one of which struck our canoe with such violence that I thought that it was a great tree, about to break the canoe to pieces. On another occasion, we saw on the water a monster with the head of a tiger, a sharp nose like that of a wildcat, with whiskers and straight, erect ears; the head was gray and the neck quite black; but we saw no more creatures of this sort. When we cast our nets into the water we caught sturgeon, and a very extraordinary kind of fish. . . .

Discovering Buffalo

When we reached the parallel of 41 degrees 28 minutes, following the same direction, we found that turkeys had taken the place of game; and the pisikious, or wild cattle, that of the other animals.

We call them "wild cattle," because they are very similar to our domestic cattle. They are not longer, but are nearly as large again, and more corpulent. When our people killed one, three persons had much difficulty in moving it. The head is very large; The forehead is flat, and a foot and a half wide between the horns, which are exactly like those of our oxen, but black and much larger. Under the neck they have a sort of large dewlap, which hangs down; and on the back is a rather high hump. The whole of the head, the neck, and a portion of the shoulders, are covered with a thick mane like that of horses; It forms a crest a foot long, which makes them hideous, and, falling over their eyes, prevents them from seeing what is before them. The remainder of the body is covered with a heavy coat of curly hair, almost like that of our sheep, but much stronger and thicker. It falls off in summer, and the skin becomes as soft as velvet. At that season, the savages use the hides for making fine robes, which they paint in various colors. . . .

Monsters and Rapids

While skirting some rocks, which by their height and length inspired awe, we saw upon one of them two painted monsters which at first made us afraid, and upon which the boldest savages dare not long rest their eyes. They are as large as a calf; they have horns on their heads like those of deer, a horrible look, red eyes, a beard like a tiger's, a face somewhat like a man's, a body covered with scales, and so long a tail that it winds all around the body, passing above the head and going back between the legs, ending in a fish's tail. Green, red, and black are the three colors composing the picture. Moreover, these 2 monsters are so well painted that we cannot believe that any savage is their author; for good painters in France would find it difficult to paint so well,—and, besides, they are so high up on the rock that it is difficult to reach that place conveniently to paint them. Here is approximately the shape of these monsters, As we have faithfully copied it.

A Way to the Southern Sea?

While conversing about these monsters, sailing quietly in clear and calm water, we heard the noise of a rapid, into which we were about to run. I have seen nothing more dreadful. An accumulation of large and entire trees, branches, and floating islands, was issuing from the mouth of the river pekistanoui [Missouri River, which joins the Mississippi near St. Louis], with such impetuosity that we could not without great danger risk passing through it. So great was the agitation that the water was very muddy, and could not become clear.

Pekitanouï is a river of considerable size, coming from the northwest, from a great distance; and it discharges into the Missisipi. There are many villages of savages along this river, and I hope by its means to discover the vermillion or California sea.

Judging from the direction of the course of the Missisipï, if it continue the same way, we think that it discharges into the Mexican gulf. It would be a great advantage to find the river leading to the southern sea, toward California; and, as I have said, this is what I hope to do by means of the Pekitanouï, according to the reports made to me by the savages. From them I have learned that, by ascending this river for 5 or 6 days, one reaches a fine prairie, 20 or 30 leagues long. This must be crossed in a northwesterly direction, and it terminates at another small river,—on which one may embark, for it is not very difficult to transport canoes through so fine a country as that prairie. This 2nd river flows toward the southwest for 10 or 15 leagues, after which it enters a lake, small and deep, which flows toward the West, where it falls into the sea. I have hardly any doubt that it is the vermillion sea, and I do not despair of discovering it some day. . . .

A Tense Meeting

While drifting down with the current . . . we perceived on land some savages armed with guns, who awaited us. I at once offered them my plumed calumet [a ceremonial pipe used as a sign of peace], while our Frenchmen prepared for defense, but delayed firing, that the savages might be the first to discharge their guns. I spoke to them in Huron, but they answered me by a word which seemed to me a declaration of war against us. However, they were as frightened as we were; and what we took for a signal for battle was an invitation that they gave us to draw near, that they might give us food. We therefore landed, and entered their cabins, where they offered us meat from wild cattle and bear's grease, with white plums, which are very good. They have guns, hatchets, hoes, knives, beads, and flasks of double glass, in which they put their powder. They wear their hair long, and tattoo their bodies after the Hiroquois [Iroquois] fashion. The women wear head-dresses and garments like those of the Huron women. They assured us that we were no more than ten days' journey from the sea; that they bought cloth and all other goods from the Europeans who lived to the east, that these Europeans had rosaries and pictures; that they played upon instruments; that some of them looked like me, and had been received by these savages kindly. Nevertheless, I saw none who seemed to have received any instruction in the faith; I gave them as much as I could, with some medals.

This news animated our courage, and made us paddle with fresh ardor. . . .

Unfriendlies Ahead

We embarked early on the following day, with our interpreter; a canoe containing ten savages went a short distance ahead of us. When we arrived within half a league of the Akamsea [the Arkansas River, which joins the Mississippi only a few hundred miles from the Gulf of Mexico], we saw two canoes coming to meet us. He who commanded stood upright, holding in his hand the calumet, with which he made various signs, according to the custom of the country. He joined us, singing very agreeably, and gave us tobacco to smoke; after that, he offered us sagamité, and bread made of indian corn, of which we ate a little. He then preceded us, after making us a sign to follow him slowly. A place had been prepared for us under the scaffolding of the chief of the warriors; it was clean, and carpeted with fine rush mats. Upon these we were made to sit, having around us the elders, who were nearest to us; after them, the warriors; and, finally, all the common people in a crowd. We fortunately found there a young man who understood Ilinois much better than did the interpreter whom we had brought from Mitchigamea. Through him, I spoke at first to the whole assembly by the usual presents. They admired what I said to them about God and the mysteries of our holy faith. They manifested a great desire to retain me among them, that I might instruct them.

We afterward asked them what they knew about the sea. They replied that we were only ten days' journey from it— we could have covered the distance in 5 days; that they were not acquainted with the nations who dwelt there, because their enemies prevented them from trading with those Europeans; that the hatchets, knives, and beads that we saw were sold to them partly by nations from the east, and partly by an Ilinois village situated at four days' journey from their village westward. They also told us that the savages with guns whom we had met were their enemies, who barred their way to the sea, and prevented them from becoming acquainted with the Europeans, and from carrying on any trade with them; that, moreover, we exposed ourselves to great dangers by going farther, on account of the continual forays of their enemies along the river,—because, as they had guns and were very warlike, we could not without manifest danger proceed down the river, which they constantly occupy. . . .

Turning Back

Monsieur Jolliet and I held another council, to deliberate upon what we should do—whether we should push on, or remain content with the discovery which we had made. After attentively considering that we were not far from the Gulf of Mexico, the basin of which is at the latitude of 31 degrees 60 minutes, while we were at 33 degrees 40 minutes, we judged that we could not be more than 2 or 3 days' journey from it; and that, beyond a doubt, the Missisipi river discharges into the Florida or Mexican gulf, and not to the east in Virginia, whose sea-coast is at 34 degrees latitude,— which we had passed, without, however, having as yet reached the sea,—or to the west in California, because in that case our route would have been to the west, or the west-southwest, whereas we had always continued it toward the south. We further considered that we exposed ourselves to the risk of losing the results of this voyage, of which we could give no information if we proceeded to fling ourselves into the hands of the Spaniards who, without doubt, would at least have detained us as captives. Moreover, we saw very plainly that we were not in a condition to resist savages allied to the Europeans, who were numerous, and expert in firing guns, and who continually infested the lower part of the river. Finally, we had obtained all the information that could be desired in regard to this discovery. All these reasons induced us to decide upon returning; this we announced to the savages, and, after a day's rest, made our preparations for it.

Chronology

1488
Portuguese navigator Bartolomeu Dias reaches the Cape of Good Hope, thus proving that it is possible to reach the Indian Ocean from the Atlantic.

1492
Christopher Columbus's first voyage encounters land in the modern-day Bahamas.

1493
Columbus begins his second expedition, in which he would further explore the Caribbean, including the islands of Española, Puerto Rico, Jamaica, and Cuba.

1494
Spain and Portugal sign the Treaty of Tordesillas to divide all future discoveries in the Americas between the two countries and thus exclude other European powers.

1497
John Cabot sails from England and reaches Newfoundland in North America; Vasco da Gama begins the voyage that will be the first to round the Cape of Good Hope and reach India.

1498
Columbus's third voyage reaches the South American continent off the coast of Venezuela.

1499
Amerigo Vespucci's first voyage explores the coast of South America.

1500
Pedro Álvares Cabral's Portuguese fleet bound for India finds the coast of Brazil first.

1502
Columbus's fourth and final voyage takes him to Central America and also maroons him and his men on Jamaica for one year.

1506
Christopher Columbus dies.

1512
Juan Ponce de León begins exploration of the coast of Florida and Yucatán in search of gold and slaves.

1513
Vasco Núñez de Balboa crosses the Isthmus of Panama and claims the Pacific Ocean for the king of Spain.

1519
Hernán Cortés begins the conquest of the Aztec Empire. Ferdinand Magellan launches an expedition that will circumnavigate the world and discover straits leading through southern South America.

1522
Of Magellan's crew of more than two hundred on five ships, only one vessel returns with approximately thirty men.

1524
Giovanni da Verrazzano explores the Atlantic coast of North America on behalf of France.

1528
Spanish conquistador Pánfilo de Narváez, who had participated in the bloody conquest of Cuba in 1513, leads an ill-

fated expedition to the unexplored and vast territory stretching from Florida to eastern Mexico. Four survivors, including Álvar Núñez Cabeza de Vaca, arrive at a Spanish outpost in Mexico roughly eight years later.

1532
Spaniard Francisco Pizarro begins his conquest and looting of the Incan Empire in Peru.

1534
Jacques Cartier begins his exploration of eastern Canada.

1539
Hernando de Soto leads an expedition to explore and conquer the lower south of the present-day United States.

1540
Francisco Vásquez de Coronado begins his exploration of the southwestern United States.

1542
Juan Rodríguez Cabrillo explores the coast of California in hopes of reaching Asia. Francisco de Orellana navigates the Amazon River. Bartolomé de Las Casas publishes *A Short Account of the Destruction of the Indies*, which condemns the methods used to colonize the Americas and argues for more humane treatment of native Americans.

1598
A Spanish colony is founded by Juan de Oñate near present-day Santa Fe, New Mexico.

1607
The English establish colonies at Jamestown (Virginia) and Sagadahoc (Maine). The latter is abandoned within two years.

1608

Samuel de Champlain founds a French settlement at Quebec.

1609

Henry Hudson explores the Hudson River for the Dutch Republic.

1672

Fur trader Louis Jolliet and Jesuit missionary Jacques Marquette explore the Mississippi River.

For Further Research

Silvio A. Bedini, ed., *Christopher Columbus and the Age of Exploration: An Encyclopedia.* New York: Da Capo, 1998.

Richard E. Bohlander, ed., *World Explorers and Discoverers.* New York: Da Capo, 1998.

Herbert Eugene Bolton, ed., *Spanish Exploration in the Southwest, 1542–1706.* New York: Barnes & Noble, 1963.

Daniel J. Boorstin, *The Discoverers.* New York: Random House, 1983.

Paul S. Boyer et al., eds., *The Enduring Vision: A History of the American People.* Boston: Houghton Mifflin, 2000.

Fredi Chiappelli, ed., *First Images of America: The Impact of the New World on the Old.* Berkeley and Los Angeles: University of California Press, 1976.

Stephen Clissold, *The Seven Cities of Cíbola.* New York: Clarkson N. Potter, 1962.

James P. Delgado, *Across the Top of the World: The Quest for the Northwest Passage.* New York: Checkmark Books, 1999.

Martin A. Favata and José B. Fernández, trans., *The Account: Álvar Núñez Cabeza de Vaca's "Relación."* Houston: Arte Público, 1993.

William W. Fitzhugh et al., eds., *Vikings: The North Atlantic Saga.* Washington, DC: Smithsonian Institution, 2000.

Robert H. Fuson, *Juan Ponce de León and the Spanish Discovery of Puerto Rico and Florida.* Blacksburg, VA: McDonald & Woodward, 2000.

Ann Graham Gaines, *Hernando de Soto and the Spanish Search for Gold in World History.* Berkeley Heights, NJ: Enslow, 2002.

Edward J. Goodman, *The Explorers of South America.* New York: Macmillan, 1972.

Stephen Greenblatt, *Marvelous Possessions: The Wonder of the New World.* Chicago: University of Chicago Press, 1991.

John R. Hale and the Editors of Time-Life Books, *Age of Exploration.* New York: Time, 1966.

Raymond John Howgego, *Encyclopedia of Exploration to 1800.* Sydney, Australia: Hordern House, 2003.

Alvin M. Josephy Jr., *Five Hundred Nations: An Illustrated History of North American Indians.* New York: Knopf, 1994.

Bartolomé de Las Casas, *History of the Indies.* Trans. and ed. by Andrée Collard. New York: Harper & Row, 1971.

Miguel Leon-Portilla, ed., *The Broken Spears: The Aztec Account of the Conquest of Mexico.* Boston: Beacon, 1962.

Milton Meltzer, *Columbus and the World Around Him.* New York: Franklin Watts, 1990.

Jerald T. Milanich and Susan Milbrath, eds., *First Encounters: Spanish Explorations in the Caribbean and the United States, 1492–1570.* Gainesville: University of Florida Press, 1989.

Dan O'Sullivan, *The Age of Discovery, 1400–1550.* London: Longman, 1984.

J.H. Parry, ed., *The European Reconnaissance: Selected Documents.* New York: Harper & Row, 1968.

Kirkpatrick Sale, *The Conquest of Paradise: Christopher Columbus and the Columbian Legacy.* New York: Knopf, 1990.

Robert Silverberg, *The Longest Voyage: Circumnavigators in the Age of Discovery.* Athens: Ohio University Press, 1997.

Michael Wood, *Conquistadors*. London: BBC, 2000.

John Yewell, Chris Dodge, and Jan DeSirey, eds., *Confronting Columbus: An Anthology*. Jefferson, NC: McFarland, 1992.

Howard Zinn, *A People's History of the United States, 1492–Present*. Rev. ed. New York: HarperPerennial, 1995.

Index

African explorers, 25, 68, 69
Amazon, the
  expedition along
    battles with Indians during,
      192–93, 195–96
    dangers during, 191–92
    lack of food during, 190–91
    villages along, 193–95
    women of, 162, 196–98
Americas, the. *See* New World,
  the
ancients, the, 71
animals, 104
Antarctic Pole, 61
Antilia, 35, 162
Apache, 204
Arab seamen, 25
Arawak, 89
Asia. *See* China
Atabaliba (Inca ruler)
  contrasted with King Charles of
    Spain, 144–45
  death of, 151–52
  promising gold and silver to
    Spaniards by, 149–50
  receiving by, of Spaniards in
    peace, 145–46
  throwing Bible on the ground
    by, 146–47
  treason of, 151
Atahuallpa. *See* Atabaliba
Ayala, Pedro De, 53–54
Aztec Empire
  amazing cities of, 167–70
  destruction of, 27
  people of, 143
  Spanish conquest of
    by Cortés, 134–38

gold and, 140–41
march to Cholula and, 164–65
Montezuma meeting with
  Spanish invaders and,
  170–72
Montezuma's efforts to
  prevent, 164–66
native perspective on, 168, 169
seizing Montezuma and,
  138–40
warning on, 166
see also Mexico

Balboa, Vasco Núñez de, 18–19
accusations against, 132
denigrating by, of his
  opponents, 125
discoveries of, 126–28
leadership of, 125–26
requesting by, of slave trade for
  Native Americans, 130–31
requesting supplies and
  provisions by, 129–30
Boemia, Martin de, 59
Brazil, 21
  Cabral's arrival on, 92–93
  future profits in, 100–101
  Magellan's arrival in, 57–58
buffalo, 204–205, 218–19

Cabeza de Vaca, Álvar Núñez,
  162, 173
Cabot, John, 22, 47
  letters on expedition by, 48–54
  response to news of discovery
    by, 23–24
Cabral, Pedro Álvares, 21
  arrival of, in Brazil, 92–93

encounters of, with Native
Americans, 93–94, 95–100
on future profits in Brazil,
100–101
mass and sermon during
expedition of, 94–95
Cabrillo, Juan Rodríquez, 72, 73
death of, 77
expedition of
dangers during, 16–17
encountering native peoples
during, 73–75
return home and, 78–79
storm during, 75–78
taking possession of port and,
73
Caminha, Pedro Vaz de, 92
Canada, 22, 183
Caribbean islands, 26
Carlo, Don, 59
Cartagena, Johan de, 58
Cartier, Jacques, 22, 181
distrust between Native
Americans and, 185–86
kidnapping of Indian chief and,
188–89
Native Americans and, 186–88
search for Saquenay and,
183–84
Carvajal, Gaspar de, 190
Catarax (Indian chief), 207–208
cattle, 204–205
Cazada, Gaspar de, 58, 59
Champlain, Samuel de, 210
Charles V (king of Spain),
144–45
charts, sea, 16–17
China
explorers of, 24
letters on attempted expedition
to, 48–54
Verrazzano's expedition and, 71
Cholula (Mexico), 164–65
Christianity

goal of spreading, 81–82
Native Americans as easy
converts to, 98–100
proclamation to Native
Americans on, 96, 97
see also religion
Christians
as feared by Native Americans,
177–78
quarrels among, 179–80
see also Europeans
City of Mexico, 169–70
Cocha, Anthonio, 58
Columbus, Christopher, 37, 83
deceiving his crew, 40
different claims on greatness of,
44, 45
discovering land by, 43–46
exploiting Native Americans for
profit and, 88, 89
exploration of islands by, 84–85
exploration prior to, 24–25, 68,
69
help from native peoples to, 26
heroic status of, 14–15
on Native Americans, 85–86,
89–91
native people welcoming,
117–18
navigation methods of, 16
objectives of, 18, 20–21
reaching Grand Canary island
by, 38–39
response to news of discovery
by, 24
searching for land and, 39–43
taking Native Americans by
force and, 86–87
town erected by, 87–88
unfavorable crew of, 38
voyages of, 90
worrying over crew of, 41–42
compass, 15
Conceptione (ship), 60, 61

Coronado, Francisco Vásquez de, 162–63

Cortés, Hernán, 19, 133
  description by, of Temixtitan, 142–43
  destruction of Aztec civilization under, 27
  meeting of, with Montezuma, 171–72
  reliance of, on Native Americans, 25–26
  warning by, 165

Cuba, 113

Dauphine (ship), 64

Day, John, 52–53

dead reckoning, 16

de Soto, Hernando, 153
  attack on Native Americans under, 155–56
  demanding obedience by, from Native Americans, 157
  exploits of, 154
  greed of, 157–58
  is lost during Florida expedition, 159

Dias, Bartolomeu, 21

Dias, Diogo, 95

Díaz del Castillo, Bernal, 122, 164

diseases, 123

Donna-cona (Indian leader), 182, 184, 188–89

El Dorado, legend of, 162

encomienda system, 27–28, 89

England
  Cabot's expedition and, 48–54
  exploration by, 21–22
  North American colonies of, 200

Escovedo, Rodrigo de, 46

Europeans
  attitude of, toward native peoples, 28–29

battle techniques and resources of, 122–23
  benefits brought by native peoples to, 29–30
  debate over treatment of Native Americans among, 82
  diversity of experiences among, 128, 129
  as feared by native peoples, 74–75
  goal of monarchs and, 19–22
  power struggles among, 124–33
  treatment of native peoples by, 30–31
  see also Christians; explorers

exploration
  before Columbus, 24–25, 68, 69
  by Cabot, 48–54
  by Cabrillo, 73–79
  early explorers kindling an interest in, 35
  finding Straits of Magellan and, 56–62
  non-European contributions to, 25–26
  seventeenth-century, 31–32
  in Spanish Southwest, 203–209
  unknown dangers in, 35–36
  unreliability of maps and charts for, 16–17
  by Verrazzano, 64–71
  wind direction and, 17
  see also Columbus, Christopher; explorers; New World, the

exploration narratives
  as heroic tales, 13–15
  information found in, 12, 32
  as intelligence reports, 23–24
  monster tales in, 36
  omissions in, 12–13, 24, 28, 29
  sources of, 12

explorers
  African, 25, 68, 69
  Asian, 24

dangers of sea travel for, 16–18
help by Native Americans to,
 25–26
heroic status of, 13–15
incomplete knowledge of
 geography and, 15
navigation methods of, 15–16
objectives of, 18–19
reporting of, to patrons and
 monarchs, 18–19
Scandinavian, 24–25, 69
scramble for information
 among, 22–24
see also Europeans; exploration;
 names of individual explorers

Ferdinand (king of Spain), 81
Ferrelo, Bartolome, 77
Florida
 legends and myths inspiring
 expeditions in, 162, 163
 Spanish attack on, 154–60
 Spanish presence in, 200, 201
France
 allied by Native Americans in
 battle with Iroquois, 211–15
 Cartier and, 182–89
 expedition of, along the
 Mississippi River, 216–23
 exploration by, 22
 fur-trading posts by, 200
 Louisiana Purchase and, 201

Galveston Islands, 174
geography, 15–16
gold and silver
 in Amazon villages, 195
 Amazon women and, 197–98
 Balboa's discovery of, 126–27
 conquest of Aztec Empire and,
 140–41, 166
 as motivation for interior
 expeditions, 162
 Native American slave labor

and, 88, 89
 settlers needing food over, 126
 Spaniards attacking Native
 American leader over, 116–17
 Spanish looting of Incan Empire
 and, 149–51
Gomes, Stefan, 60–61
Grand Canary Island, 38–39
Greenblatt, Stephen, 32, 128, 129
Guacanagarí (Native American
 leader), 117, 118
Gutierrez, Pero, 45–46

Haiti, 89
Hale, John R., 17
Hanke, Lewis, 96, 97
Henry VII (king of England), 22
Henry the Navigator, 35
historians, 14–15
Hy Brasil, 35

Incan Empire
 Atabaliba's desire for peace in,
 145–46
 Atabaliba's treason and death
 and, 151–52
 looting of, 148–52
 slaughter of people in, 147–48
Indians. *See* Native Americans
indigenous people. *See* Native
 Americans
Iroquois, 210
Isabella (queen of Spain), 81
Iztapalapa (Aztec Empire), 167

Jamaica, 113
Japan, 50
Jolliet, Louis, 216

Kansas, 163, 207–208

Las Casas, Bartolomé de, 37, 109
latitude-longitude measurements,
 15–16

legends, 162–63
Leon-Portilla, Miguel, 29
Lopez, Affonso, 93

Magellan, Ferdinand, expedition of
  in Brazil, 57–58
  desertion of ship during, 60–61
  discovery of straits during, 59–60
  going toward Antarctic Pole during, 61
  hardships during, 56–57, 62
  struggle against mutineers during, 58–59
maps, 16–17
Marble, Samuel D., 68, 69
Marquette, Jacques, 31–32, 200–201, 216
Mexico
  decline in native population of, 26
  plantation system in, 141–42
  see also Aztec Empire
Mississippi River, 216–23
Mohawk, John, 44
monarchs
  explorers reporting to, 18–19
  goals of, 19–22
Montaigne, Michel Eyquem de, 30
Montezuma
  admirable attributes of, 143
  Cortés's promise on, 134
  meeting of, with Spaniards, 170–72
  request of, to not invade Aztec Empire, 138–39, 165–66
  seizing of, 139
  as vassal, 139–40
  see also Aztec Empire
Morison, Samuel Eliot, 14–15, 69
Muslims, 81
mythical lands, 35, 162–63

Native Americans
  as absent or distorted in exploration narratives, 28, 29
  aiding French in battle with Iroquois, 211–15
  along the Amazon River, 191–93, 194, 195
  asking of, to be cured by Spanish, 176
  Balboa's treatment of, 125–26
  battle techniques and resources of, 122–23
  benefits to Europe through, 29–30
  as brute creatures, 69–70
  Cabrillo's expedition and, 73–74
  Christianity and, 91, 96–100, 177–79
  Columbus describing, 85–86, 89–91
  Columbus taking of, by force, 86–87
  Columbus welcomed by, 117–18
  communication with, 70, 93–94
  conquest of Aztecs and, 123, 134, 135–36
  contributions of, and help to explorers, 25–26
  customs of, 105–106
  depopulation of, 25, 112–13
  devastation brought to, 25–27
  distrust of, 185–86
  dwellings of, 105
  European attitudes toward, 28–29
  European treatment of, 30–31, 82
  fear and timidity in, 95–96
  fear by, of Europeans, 74–75
  food of, 105
  friendliness of, 65–66, 67–68
  helping Spanish, 174

kidnapping of chiefs and,
154–55, 188–89
kingdoms of, 115–16, 117, 118
as lacking a religion, 70–71
meal of, with explorers, 97–98
murder of leader and, 116–17,
118–19
natural goodness of, 111–12
pearls of, 127
perspective of, on conquest of
Aztec Empire, 168, 169
physical description of, 57–58,
93, 104–105
request for slave trade of,
130–31
resistance by, 114–15
slaughter of Incan, 146–48
slave labor by, 27–28, 88, 89,
119–20
Southwest, 204, 205–207,
208–209
Spaniards quarreling with
Christians over, 179–80
Spanish attack on, in Florida,
153–60
Spanish greed and, 113–14
Spanish policy and practice
toward, 110–11
trade with, 57, 70, 86, 182,
187–88
travel of, with Spaniards,
176–77
on voyage with French
explorers, 183, 184
as a warlike people, 106–107
women, 90–91, 106
navigation methods, 15–16
Newfoundland, 25, 181
New Mexico, 200, 203
New World, the
Cabrillo's expedition in, 73–79
devastation in, 26–28
legends and myths inspiring
expeditions in, 162–63

power struggles in, 125–32
Vespucci's expedition to,
103–108
see also exploration; North
America; South America
Niquesa, Diego de, 125, 129
North America
de Soto's expedition to, 154–60
European presence in, 200–201
French expedition along the
Mississippi River of, 216–23
inland exploration of the
Southwest of, 203–209
seventeenth-century, 31–32
traveling along the St. Lawrence
River of, 182–89
Verrazzano's expedition to,
64–71
see also New World, the

Ojeda, Alonso de, 125, 129
Old World. *See* Europeans
Oñate, Juan de, 31, 163, 202, 203
Orellana, Francisco de, 13–14,
162, 190
Oviedo y Valdés, Gonzalo
Fernández de, 153

Pasqualigo, Lorenzo, 48
Pigafetta, Antonio, 55
Pinzón, Martín Alonzo, 38, 39, 42
plants, 104
Polo, Marco, 35
Ponce de León, Juan, 163
Portugal, 20, 21
Cabral's expedition in Brazil
and, 92–101
as dominant sea power, 35
Magellan's expedition and,
56–62
printing, 23
Puerto Rico, 113

Quintero, Christopher, 38

Quivira, Kansas, 163, 207–208

Rascon, Gomez, 38
religion
  Columbus's goal of converting
    natives and, 91
  as justification for treatment of
    native people, 27–28, 81
  native peoples as lacking, 70–71
  see also Christianity
Requerimiento, the (the
  Requirement), 96, 97

Saguenay, 183–84
Sanchez, Rodrigo, 46
Sancto Anthonio (ship), 60–61
Scandinavian exploration, 24–25,
  69
Seven Cities of Cibola, 162–63
Siera Leona, 56
silver. *See* gold and silver
slave trade, 130–31
Soncino, Raimondo De Raimondi
  De, 49–52
South America
  exploration along the Amazon
    River in, 190–98
  looting of Incan Empire in,
    148–52
  see also Aztec Empire; Brazil;
    New World, the
Southwest, the
  Apache in, 204
  buffalo in, 204–205
  crops in, 208
  food during journey in, 204
  Native Americans of, 205–207
  preparing for journey to, 203
  returning from journey to,
    208–209
  settlements in, 207–208
Spain/Spaniards
  appeal to change policy toward
    Native Americans by, 110–11

Cabrillo's expedition and,
    73–79
  conquest of Aztec Empire by,
    134–43, 164–72
  exploration of the Southwest by,
    203–209
  genocide of Native Americans
    by, 112–13
  goal of spreading Christianity
    by, 81–82
  goals of monarchs in, 20–21
  looting of Incan Empire by,
    148–52
  motives for interior expeditions
    by, 162–63
  Native American resistance
    against, 114–15
  quarrels among, 179–80
  raft voyage and, 174–75
  traveling with Native
    Americans, 176–79
  wickedness and greed of,
    113–14, 157–58, 159–60
  see also Columbus, Christopher;
    Europeans
Spanish Inquisition, 81
spices, 50–51, 91
St. Brendan Isle, 35
St. Elmo's fire, 56–57
St. Lawrence River, 182–89, 200

Temixtitan (Aztec Empire),
    142–43
Tlascala (Aztec Empire), 137–38
Tlaxcalans, 25
Tordesillas, Treaty of, 21
trade
  between Africa and South
    America, 68
  between explorers and native
    peoples, 57, 70, 86, 182,
    187–88
  in Mexico, 142–43
  of spices, 50–51

Triana, Rodrigo de, 45

Verrazzano, Giovanni da, 22, 63, 64–71
Vespucci, Amerigo, 14, 102, 103–108
Vikings, the, 69

weaponry, 122
women
  Amazon, 162, 196–98

Native American
  childbirth and, 106
  Columbus describing, 90–91
  marriage and, 106

Xeres, Francisco de, 144

Yanez, Vincent, 46

Zinn, Howard, 88, 89